THE ULTIMATE
PHILADELPHIA FLYERS
TRIVIA BOOK

A Collection of Amazing Trivia Quizzes and Fun Facts for Die-Hard Flyers Fans!

Ray Walker

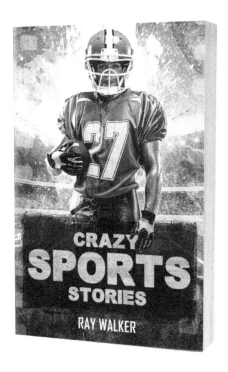

CONTENTS

INTRODUCTION

Hockey typically brings out passion and loyalty in fans, and supporters of the Philadelphia Flyers are among the most vocal and fiercely passionate in the NHL. They cheer excitedly for their team but aren't afraid to show their disappointment if the club doesn't play up to par.

The Flyers have been entertaining fans since the league doubled in size in 1967 and the team made history when it became the first expansion franchise to win the Stanley Cup. There have been many high points in the City of Brotherly Love since the Flyers came to town with enough low points to keep them humble.

Some of the NHL's most famous players and coaches have represented the organization since day one. Nineteen former Flyers are already enshrined in the Hockey Hall of Fame, and there's no end in sight.

This trivia and fact book about the Flyers celebrates the club's history from inception to the end of the 2019-20 regular season. It looks back at exactly what makes the team tick and why Flyers fans are so passionate about their team.

Each of the 15 chapters deals with a specific topic in franchise history and is meant to challenge your skills as a fan of the team. You'll be able to test your knowledge by answering the 20 multiple-choice or true-false questions in each chapter. The answers are provided on a separate page to make sure you're not tempted to peek. You can then refresh your memory by reading through the 10 interesting "Did You Know" facts about the Flyers.

For some fans, the book will bring back fond and not-so-fond memories, while others will read it for entertainment purposes or to educate themselves about the famous Philadelphia Flyers franchise.

The book also presents an excellent opportunity to challenge fellow supporters to see who really does know the most about the club.

Whatever your reason is for checking out the book, you'll be sure to reaffirm your love for your favorite NHL team while doing so.

The statistics and information gathered for the book are up to date through the conclusion of the 2019-20 NHL regular season. There are sure to be many more highlights for the Flyers over the coming years, and more history will surely be made in the future. For now, this book has all the information required to make you an up-to-date expert on the Philadelphia Flyers.

CHAPTER 1:

ORIGINS & HISTORY

QUIZ TIME!

1. The Philadelphia Flyers played their first-ever regular-season NHL game in which season?

    a. 1970-71

    b. 1967-68

    c. 1968-69

    d. 1965-66

2. Which division did the Flyers play in during their first seven seasons?

    a. West

    b. Atlantic

    c. Metropolitan

    d. East

3. The Flyers were the first team not part of the "Original Six" to win a Stanley Cup.

    a. True

    b. False

4. There have been 21 coaches in Flyers history. Who was the first?

    a. Vic Stasiuk
    b. Fred Shero
    c. Pat Quinn
    d. Keith Allen

5. Who did the Flyers lose to in their NHL debut?

    a. California Seals
    b. Detroit Red Wings
    c. Toronto Maple Leafs
    d. Los Angeles Kings

6. The Flyers were a part of the NHL first expansion group, dubbed the "Second Six." Which of the following teams was not part of that expansion?

    a. Los Angeles Kings
    b. California Golden Seals
    c. New York Islanders
    d. St. Louis Blues

7. Who scored the Flyers' first hat trick?

    a. Jim Johnson
    b. Andre Lacroix
    c. Rosaire Paiement
    d. Leon Rochefort

8. At the conclusion of the 2019-20 season, the Flyers held the 3rd best all-time point percentage in the NHL. What is that percentage?

a. 55.7%

b. 52.9%

c. 57.5%

d. 60%

9. Through 2019, the Flyers made the playoffs 49 times.

a. True

b. False

10. In the 1972-73 season, which player became the then-youngest captain in the NHL?

a. Bill Barber

b. Bobby Clarke

c. Rick MacLeish

d. Bill Clement

11. What was the name of Philadelphia's first NHL team in 1930-31?

a. Philadelphia Quakers

b. Philadelphia Pirates

c. Philadelphia Liberty Bell

d. Philadelphia Arrows

12. During that 1930-31 season, Philadelphia posted a wins-losses-ties record of 4-36-4, which stands as one of the worst seasons in NHL history.

a. True

b. False

13. How many times have the Flyers reached the Stanley Cup Finals?

a. 7

b. 5

c. 10

d. 8

14. The Flyers were the first team to wear which article of equipment in the NHL in the 1981 season?

    a. Neck protectors

    b. Helmet visors

    c. Cooperalls pants

    d. Ear protectors

15. The 2006-07 season saw a record in franchise worsts for the Flyers, including how many losses?

    a. 50

    b. 48

    c. 40

    d. 39

16. Before the Flyers' infamous mascot Gritty took the hockey world by storm, who was the Flyers' first mascot?

    a. Slapshot

    b. Phlex

    c. Bruiser

    d. Phil the Flyer

17. Who made up the broadcasting duo for the Flyers' inaugural season?

    a. Gene Hart and Larry Zeidel

    b. Gene Hart and Don Earle

c. Stu Nahan and Bill White

d. Stu Nahan and Gene Hart

18. The first Flyers captain in franchise history was:

a. Ed Van Impe

b. Lou Angotti

c. Jean-Guy Gendron

d. Leon Rochefort

19. Which of the following accidents to the Spectrum forced the Flyers to play the remainder of their home games at a neutral rink in 1967-68?

a. The roof was blown off in a storm.

b. The arena flooded, causing extensive damage to the team locker rooms.

c. The air conditioner broke, resulting in less than favorable ice conditions.

d. The arena's Jumbotron fell to the ice before the start of a game.

20. Who was the first player selected by the Flyers in the 1967 NHL Expansion Draft?

a. Doug Favell

b. Serge Bernier

c. Bernie Parent

d. Al Sarault

QUIZ ANSWERS

1. B – 1967-68

2. A – West

3. A – True

4. D – Keith Allen

5. A – California Seals

6. C – New York Islanders

7. D – Leon Rochefort

8. C – 57.5%

9. B – False

10. B – Bobby Clarke

11. A – Philadelphia Quakers

12. A – True

13. D – 8

14. C – Cooperalls pants

15. B – 48

16. A – Slapshot

17. D – Stu Nahan and Gene Hart

18. B – Lou Angotti

19. A – The roof was blown off in a storm.

20. C – Bernie Parent

DID YOU KNOW?

1. The NHL doubled in size in the 1967-68 season when the "Original Six" teams, as they were known, were joined by six newcomers. This meant the Original Six now had to deal with the California Seals, Philadelphia Flyers, St. Louis Blues, Pittsburgh Penguins, Los Angeles Kings, and Minnesota North Stars. The Original Six teams made up the East Division and the expansion franchises made up the West Division.

2. Philadelphia won back-to-back Stanley Cups in 1974 and 1975 and became the first expansion franchise to hoist the trophy. They lost in the Stanley Cup Final in 1976 and were also beaten in the Final in 1980, 1985, 1987, 1997, and 2010. The team has led the NHL in regular-season points on three occasions: 1974-75, 1979-80, and 1984-85, before the President's Trophy was presented to the squad with the most regular-season points.

3. The Flyers are based in Philadelphia, Pennsylvania. The only other NHL team in the state is the Pittsburgh Penguins. The Flyers compete in the Metropolitan Division of the Eastern Conference. Philadelphia's home rink has always been located on Broad Street on the south side of the city. Their first rink was the Spectrum, where they played from 1967 to 1996, and they now call the Wells Fargo Center home. Going into the 2019-20 season, the Flyers had made the playoffs 39 times.

4. The Wells Fargo Center opened in 1996 and is also the home of the National Basketball Association's Philadelphia 76ers and the Philadelphia Wings lacrosse team of the National Lacrosse League. The local area, known as the South Philadelphia Sports Complex, also includes Lincoln Financial Field, Xfinity Live, and Citizens Bank Park. The Wells Fargo Center was originally to be named Spectrum II. Its former names were CoreStates Center, First Union Center, and the Wachovia Center.

5. The franchise is owned by the Comcast Spectacor company, which also owns the Wells Fargo Center and the Global Spectrum and Comcast SportsNet corporations. Ed Snider, who passed away in 2016, was the chairman of Comcast and also used to own the Philadelphia 76ers NBA team. In addition, he was a part-owner of the National Football League's Philadelphia Eagles.

6. Philadelphia actually had an NHL team in 1930-31. This happened when the Pittsburgh Pirates found themselves in financial difficulty and moved to Philadelphia. They became the Philadelphia Quakers and played their home games at The Arena at Market and 46th Streets. The Quakers boasted a 19-year-old rookie named Syd Howe, who would be inducted into the Hockey Hall of Fame. Their coach J. Cooper Smeaton also wound up in the Hall following a later career as a referee.

7. All of the 1967-68 expansion teams filled their rosters via the 1967 NHL Expansion Draft, with each club choosing 20

players. Philadelphia ended up with some fine talent, such as goaltenders Bernie Parent and Doug Favell, as well as Joe Watson, Lou Angotti, Ed Van Impe, Bill Sutherland, Gary Dornhoefer, and Leon Rochefort.

8. Philadelphia bought an American Hockey League (AHL) team, the Quebec Aces, in the early days and also stocked their club with talent from that squad, including several French-Canadian players who were featured on early Philadelphia rosters, such as Rosaire Paiement, Serge Bernier, Andre Lacroix, Simon Nolet, and Jean-Guy Gendron. The Flyers' minor-league affiliates are now the Lehigh Valley Phantoms of the AHL and the Reading Royals of the East Coast Hockey League.

9. The Flyers' first NHL game was on the road against the California Seals on October 11, 1967, when they were trounced 5-1. Their first victory was by a 2-1 score in St. Louis over the Blues a week later. The Flyers' home debut was a bit of a disappointment as just 7,812 fans showed up on October 19. They got to celebrate, though, as they edged the Pittsburgh Penguins 1-0.

10. Philadelphia won the West Division in their inaugural season with a wins-losses-ties record of 31-32-11. They went 17-13-7 at home and 14-19-4 on the road. They were 11th in the league in goals scored, with 173, and a very respectable 3rd best in goals against at 179. Oddly enough, the roof of their home rink was partly blown off in a storm, and the team's last seven home games were played on the

road. Things didn't go too well in the playoffs, though, as St. Louis eliminated them in seven games in the 1st round.

CHAPTER 2:

JERSEYS & NUMBERS

QUIZ TIME!

1. What are the Flyers' primary jersey colors?

    a. Orange, grey, and white

    b. Gold, black, and orange

    c. Orange, red, and white

    d. Orange, black, and white

2. Which number has been most commonly worn by Flyers players?

    a. 23
    b. 15
    c. 7
    d. 40

3. Six players have had their jersey numbers retired by the Flyers organization.

    a. True
    b. False

4. The number 16 has been worn only by Bobby Clarke and which other player?

   a. Bill Clement
   b. Lou Angotti
   c. Claude LaForge
   d. Bill Sutherland

5. Eric Lindros was the only Flyer to wear which double number during his eight years with the team?

   a. 66
   b. 22
   c. 88
   d. 77

6. The Winter Classic and Stadium Series Games have generated many unique jerseys. How many unique jerseys have the Flyers worn during these special series games?

   a. 1
   b. 5
   c. 2
   d. 4

7. The design of the Flyers' logo is intended to represent which of the following attributes?

   a. Speed
   b. Strength
   c. Aggression
   d. Skill

8. In which season did the Flyers change their home jersey color from white to black?

   a. 2007-08
   b. 2001-02
   c. 2006-07
   d. 2002-03

9. Bernie Parent's number 1 has been retired. What other number did the Hall-of-Famer wear as a Flyer?

   a. 35
   b. 31
   c. 30
   d. 33

10. Which of the following players did NOT wear 20 in 1968 for the Flyers?

    a. Jean-Guy Gendron
    b. Rosaire Paiement
    c. Dick Cherry
    d. Keith Wright

11. The stripes down the shoulders of the Flyers' jerseys are intended to be racing strips.

    a. True
    b. False

12. Seven players have worn 7 for the Flyers.

    a. True
    b. False

13. Current Flyers captain Claude Giroux wears which number?

    a. 39
    b. 28
    c. 29
    d. 27

14. For their 50th season, what special modification did the Flyers make to their alternate jersey to honor the occasion?

    a. The logo was colored solid gold.
    b. The jersey included 50 pinstripes, one for each season in the league.
    c. The logo was altered to look like a 5 and 0.
    d. The numbers and trim were fashioned gold.

15. What is the highest jersey number donned by a Flyer?

    a. 95
    b. 90
    c. 92
    d. 97

16. Despite his fame for being the toughest netminder and franchise leader in wins, Ron Hextall's number has not been retired. What is that number?

    a. 17
    b. 28
    c. 27
    d. 7

17. Who is the only Flyer to wear number 78?

    a. Andrew MacDonald
    b. Sam Gagner
    c. Pierre-Edouard Bellemare
    d. Taylor Leier

18. Which number has never been worn by a member of the Flyers?

    a. 90
    b. 2
    c. 66
    d. 75

19. What number did captain Keith Primeau wear during his six seasons with the team?

    a. 26
    b. 25
    c. 7
    d. 52

20. Upon returning to the club in 2019, James van Riemsdyk wore the number 25 he wore during his first stint with the team.

    a. True
    b. False

QUIZ ANSWERS

1. D – Orange, black, and white

2. B – 15

3. A – True

4. C – Claude LaForge

5. C – 88

6. D – 4

7. A – Speed

8. A – 2007-08

9. C – 30

10. C – Dick Cherry

11. B – False

12. A – True

13. B – 28

14. D – The numbers and trim were fashioned gold.

15. D – 97

16. C – 27

17. C – Pierre-Edouard Bellemare

18. A – 90

19. B – 25

20. B – False

DID YOU KNOW?

1. Six jersey numbers have been retired by the Flyers as of 2019-20. The honor has gone to goaltender Bernie Parent (1), defensemen Mark Howe (2), and Barry Ashbee (4), and forwards Bill Barber (7), Bobby Clarke (16), and Eric Lindros (88).

2. When Philadelphia was awarded an NHL franchise in 1966, the club held a public contest to name the team and its colors. The name "Flyers" topped the ballot, and the fans voted on orange, black, and white as the colors. The city's previous NHL team, the Quakers, also wore orange and black in 1930-31. Other names considered were the Liberty Bells, Quakers, Ramblers, Bashers, Bruisers, Knights, Huskies, Raiders, Sabres, and Lancers.

3. Hockey is a game filled with tradition, which means that changes are rarely made, especially to the overall look of a hockey uniform. However, in 1981-82, the Flyers and Hartford Whalers did away with traditional hockey pants and socks and switched to long pants. These were known as Cooperalls after the company that made them. The pants went all the way to the ankles, and the teams wore them for just two seasons before reverting to traditional socks and short pants when the NHL banned Cooperalls for safety reasons.

4. The most popular jersey number with Flyers players over

the years has been 15; 37 different players wore it between 1967 and 2019. Several numbers above 59 have been worn by just one player each. The highest number worn was 97, which Jeremy Roenick chose, while the number 1 has been the lowest worn.

5. Former Philadelphia goaltender Pelle Lindbergh wore 31 during his career from 1982 to 1985. Unfortunately, Lindbergh was killed in an auto accident on November 11, 1985, at the age of 26. Lindbergh's jersey hasn't been retired, but no Flyer has worn 31 since his death.

6. The Flyers' logo design is basically a large slanted letter P in the middle of the jersey. There are four stylized wings attached to the letter, which represent speed, and an orange dot represents a hockey puck. Basically, the logo is a flying P. A *Hockey News* poll in 2008 named it the 6th best logo in the NHL.

7. The Flyers' logo was changed slightly in 2002 for the first time. The team has also worn several different versions of jerseys over the years for special occasions, such as the NHL Winter Classic and Stadium Series Games and the franchise's 50th anniversary. They have also introduced alternate and third jerseys.

8. Throughout the franchise's history to 2019-20, the Flyers have used 80 different numbers on their jerseys. Each number from 1 to 56 has been worn at least once. Nobody has worn number 57. The only numbers between 58 and 82 not worn are 63, 64, 67, 69, 71, 73, and 80.

9. The supposedly unlucky number 13 has been worn by seven different Flyers. Those who apparently aren't superstitious were Dave Michayluk, Claude Lapointe, Daniel Carcillo, Glen Metropolit, Pavel Kubina, Roman Lyubimov, and Kevin Hayes. However, nobody has worn the number on their back for longer than three years.

10. One Flyer who seemed to rarely wear his jersey during games was Dave Schultz. This is because the forward was one of the team's top enforcers from 1971 to 1976 and was often engaged in fights with opponents. Schultz served an NHL record 472 minutes in penalties in 1974-75 and had 2,292 regular-season minutes in his career. He led the league in penalty minutes in four of his nine years. Schultz also had scoring talent, though; he notched 20 goals in 1973-74.

CHAPTER 3:

FAMOUS QUOTES

QUIZ TIME!

1. Who said, "You don't have to be crazy to be goalie, but it helps."?

    a. Antero Niittymäki
    b. Ron Hextall
    c. Bernie Parent
    d. Petr Mrázek

2. Who did Bobby Clarke call "the dirtiest players I've ever seen"?

    a. Boston Bruins
    b. Russian national team
    c. New York Rangers
    d. American national team

3. Claude Giroux once said this about a referee: "I don't want to get into a 'he said, she said' with the refs... I'm the 'he.'"

    a. True
    b. False

4. "Yes, we are world champions…We beat the hell out of a machine." This was said by which Flyers coach following a win against the Red Army team?

   a. Fred Shero
   b. Pat Quinn
   c. Bob McCammon
   d. Vic Stasiuk

5. Which player said if a Flyer were to ever win the Lady Byng Trophy they should "rename it the Man Byng"?

   a. Thomas Eriksson
   b. Derrick Smith
   c. Tim Kerr
   d. Dave Brown

6. Which Flyer claimed, "I was one of the only players on the team that didn't go in the stands and I was guilty by association," about an infamous brawl with the Vancouver Canucks and their fans?

   a. Bob Taylor
   b. Barry Ashbee
   c. Don Saleski
   d. Ed Van Impe

7. Who said that the fans in Philadelphia "were either cheering for us or abusing the other team" throughout a game?

   a. Ross Lonsberry
   b. Dave Schultz

c. Bobby Clarke

d. Wayne Hillman

8. Fred Shero once remarked, "We know hockey is where we live, where we can best meet and overcome pain and wrong and death. Life is just a place where we spend time between games."

    a. True

    b. False

9. "I looked at those draft picks. I had to laugh. I knew I was better than half the guys they were picking." This was said by which player about the 1967 Expansion Draft?

    a. Forbes Kennedy

    b. Larry Zeidel

    c. Bill Sutherland

    d. Jean Gauthier

10. Following the 2018-19 season, which player said this about the team's performance: "With so many slow starts in the past, and we started slow again this year, I think we got into our heads a little too much instead of just go out there to play."?

    a. Radko Gudas

    b. Ivan Provorov

    c. Shayne Gostisbehere

    d. Jakub Voráček

11. Bobby Clarke professed that the Russian national team was "scared to death" when they arrived at the Spectrum for a 1976 match.

a. True

b. False

12. Which Flyer said this in defending himself following an accusation of a dirty hit in the 2019 Stadium Series: "It's part of the game, I'm not a dirty player, I've never been suspended in my life, I don't pick people's heads, I don't do any of that stuff."?

a. Claude Giroux

b. Wayne Simmonds

c. Oskar Lindblom

d. Michael Raffl

13. Whose development did Ron Hextall say this about in 2014 after the player was sent to the minors: "He might be the first kid I ever dealt with who knows exactly where he's at as a player and exactly where he needs to be to get better."?

a. Brandon Manning

b. Nick Cousins

c. Shayne Gostisbehere

d. Petr Straka

14. Shawn Tilger, the former senior vice-president of the Flyers said, "The fans are what make the organization."

a. True

b. False

15. Which team were the Flyers facing in the 1987 playoffs when a pre-game brawl broke out and Rick Tocchet said, "I was in the dressing room, I think I had my skates off."

a. New York Islanders

b. Edmonton Oilers

c. New York Rangers

d. Montreal Canadiens

16. Who scored 5 points in his NHL debut and had this to say about his performance: "Everything I touched seemed to go in the net either by me or by someone else."?

a. Peter Zezel

b. Eric Lindros

c. Claude Giroux

d. Al Hill

17. Following a brutal 8-2 loss in the Flyers' home opener in 2018, which goaltender said, "It's a tough game. It's not how we wanted to come out. I think every man in this room is better than that, including myself."?

a. Brian Elliott

b. Carter Hart

c. Calvin Pickard

d. Anthony Stolarz

18. Which member of the Flyers' organization said, "Sleep with one eye open, Bird," after a bad encounter with the Pittsburgh Penguins mascot?

a. Ed Snider

b. Dave Hakstol

c. Gritty

d. Ron Hextall

19. Which all-time great asked "Who the hell are you?" after Ron Hextall made a save on him in the goalie's rookie year?

    a. Wayne Gretzky
    b. Borje Salming
    c. Dave Andreychuk
    d. Bernie Federko

20. After a poor performance and being pulled for an extra man, Ron Hextall said, "The best we played was when I was on the bench. We had three-and-a-half minutes in their zone."

    a. True
    b. False

QUIZ ANSWERS

1. C – Bernie Parent

2. B – Russian national team

3. B – False

4. A – Fred Shero

5. D – Dave Brown

6. C – Don Saleski

7. C – Bobby Clarke

8. A – True

9. B – Larry Zeidel

10. D – Jakub Voráček

11. A – True

12. B – Wayne Simmonds

13. C – Shayne Gostisbehere

14. A – True

15. D – Montreal Canadiens

16. D – Al Hill

17. A – Brian Elliot

18. C – Gritty

19. A – Wayne Gretzky

20. B – False

DID YOU KNOW?

1. After the Flyers beat the Pittsburgh Penguins 4-3 in overtime of the 2019 NHL Stadium Series Game, forward Jakub Voráček was asked if the after-game handshakes surprised him considering the game was quite rough-and-tumble. Voráček replied, "What did you expect, like a brawl or something? It's a hockey game. ...That's the right thing to do in a game like that and kudos to them."

2. When Flyers defender Matt Niskanen took a puck to the face in a game in November 2019, the bloodied blueliner took 15 stitches to heal the wound and returned to the contest wearing a mask. This impressed teammate Scott Laughton who remarked, "He takes a puck in the face, he's bleeding, he stays on the ice and comes back with a cage and makes a couple plays. I said it in the intermission, he's invaluable. He's a quiet leader for us and when he speaks, people listen. He's been huge for us."

3. Former head coach Fred "The Fog" Shero was well-known for his colorful quotes. When describing captain Bobby Clarke in the 1970s, he said, "Sure, Clarke is mean. Anybody who expects to be truly great has to be mean. I'm talking about Gordie Howe, who could carve you. Or Rocket Richard. Or Milt Schmidt. They were mean. They took care of the opposition."

4. Ed Snider, the Flyers' founder and former owner,

explained why he was interested in bringing an NHL franchise to Philadelphia. "I was a sports nut, really, and I had seen a couple of hockey games, and it blew me away. Right away I thought it was the greatest spectator sport I had ever seen...the hitting, the magnificent skating."

5. When former Philadelphia great and Hall-of-Famer Eric Lindros retired in 2007 due to injuries, he remarked, "My decision to retire from professional hockey is something that I have been considering for some time and did not come easily. I will miss the day-to-day activity of being a member of a team and the camaraderie that I developed with my teammates will never be forgotten. I played with the best, I played against the best—it was a blast. It really truly was. I enjoyed myself immensely."

6. At the conclusion of the 2018-19 season, Flyers defenseman Travis Sanheim was named by his teammates as the team's most improved player. When asked how the blue line could improve, he answered, "Bigger bodies if used properly can intimidate other players and use that to your strength. It's up to us how we play and being more aggressive and assertive and physical."

7. Goaltenders are generally considered to be "off-the-wall" characters, and former Flyer Ilya Bryzgalov is no exception. The Russian netminder once said in his broken English, "OK, they fire the puck from the blue line. Chief usually yelling 'block the shot' at the defensemen. They doesn't have the goalie gear, but they have to block the

shot. So who is more crazy, me or the defensemen? Who is more weird?"

8. When speaking about former Flyers forward and supreme agitator Ken "The Rat" Linseman, former NHL head coach Glen Sonmor said, "When he was on your side, you loved him but when he wasn't, Kenny was an S.O.B." Most NHL players shared the same view of Linseman and that's why he was so effective at getting under his opponents' skin.

9. 19. For his part, Linseman said he wasn't exactly sure what the Flyers expected of him when he cracked the team's lineup in 1978. He was quoted as saying, "I was never sure if I was supposed to be a goal scorer or playmaker or just start trouble. I did take some stupid penalties."

10. Combative goalie Ron Hextall was a Flyers fan favorite, and he shared some of his thoughts on playing in net by saying, "I learned over the years that the goalie is the guy everyone notices when he makes a mistake. The first time I was booed, I'll admit it hurt. It was hard but you step back and realize it's not a personal thing. The fans just thought I wasn't playing the way they expected me to play and there's really nothing wrong with that."

CHAPTER 4:

CATCHY NICKNAMES

QUIZ TIME!

1. What infamous nickname were the Flyers given in 1972-73 by Jack Chevalier?

   a. The Flying Enforcers
   b. The Fighters of Philly
   c. Broad Street Bruisers
   d. Broad Street Bullies

2. What current Flyer player's nickname is "Ghost"?

   a. Shayne Gostisbehere
   b. Claude Giroux
   c. Kevin Hayes
   d. Justin Braun

3. Which Flyers coach was known as "The Fog"?

   a. Pat Quinn
   b. Alain Vigneault
   c. Fred Shero
   d. Craig Berube

4. Flyer Ken Linseman agitated the rest of the NHL, earning him which nickname?

   a. "The Jerk"
   b. "Ken the Critter"
   c. "The Rat"
   d. "The Pest"

5. How did Reggie Leach acquire his nickname, "The Riverton Rifle"?

   a. He practiced marksmanship in the offseason.
   b. Leach grew up in Riverton and had a rocket for a slapshot.
   c. Leach went on annual hunting trips with teammates.
   d. Leach collected antique rifles to decorate his home in Riverton.

6. Rod Brind'Amour was dubbed "Rod the Bod" because of his dedication and effort in the weight room.

   a. True
   b. False

7. Which of these Flyers captains didn't have a nickname?

   a. Chris Pronger
   b. Claude Giroux
   c. Eric Lindros
   d. Bobby Clarke

8. Which former Flyers goaltender was known as "Mr. Universe"?

a. Sergei Bobrovsky

b. Ilya Bryzgalov

c. Steve Mason

d. Martin Biron

9. Dave Schultz earned which nickname for his physical dominance on the ice?

a. "Bare-Knuckle"

b. Dave "Shudder" Schultz

c. "The Demolition Man"

d. "The Hammer"

10. Which of the following nicknames has NOT been applied to the Flyers?

a. Freddy's Philistines

b. The Fightin' Flyers

c. The Foster Home of Netminders

d. The Mean Machine

11. Phil Myers got his nickname "Leaf Eater" because his favorite animal is the giraffe.

a. True

b. False

12. Which player has given most of the nicknames to his teammates on the current Flyers roster?

a. Kevin Hayes

b. James van Riemsdyk

c. Travis Konecny

d. Jakub Voráček

13. Current captain Claude Giroux is commonly known as "G-Money."

    a. True
    b. False

14. Jakub Voráček is also known as Score-Czech, a play on the name of his home country.

    a. True
    b. False

15. What is Joel Farabee's self-proclaimed nickname?

    a. "The Buzz"
    b. "E Z Bee"
    c. "Joel Ferrari"
    d. "Young Beezer"

16. Goaltender Carter Hart's nickname is simply his name pronounced in an exaggerated Boston accent, "Cahtah Haht."

    a. True
    b. False

17. More commonly known as JVR, James van Riemsdyk has acquired what other nickname during his time in Philadelphia?

    a. "Mini Van"
    b. "Jeeves"
    c. "Goblin"
    d. "Reemer"

18. What odd animal nickname does Sean Couturier have?

    a. "The Serpent"
    b. "Lizard"
    c. "Hound Dog"
    d. "The Eagle"

19. Who was nicknamed "Mad Dog"?

    a. Bob Kelly
    b. Don Saleski
    c. Jim Watson
    d. Ron Hextall

20. Which current Flyer has the same nickname that Andre "Moose" Dupont had in the 1970s?

    a. Derek Grant
    b. Ivan Provorov
    c. Justin Braun
    d. Brian Elliot

QUIZ ANSWERS

1. D – Broad Street Bullies

2. A – Shayne Gostisbehere

3. C – Fred Shero

4. C – "The Rat"

5. B – Leach grew up in Riverton and had a rocket for a slapshot.

6. A – True

7. D – Bobby Clarke

8. B – Ilya Bryzgalov

9. D – "The Hammer"

10. C – The Foster Home of Netminders

11. B – False

12. A – Kevin Hayes

13. B – False

14. B – False

15. D – "Young Beezer"

16. A – True

17. C – "Goblin"

18. B – "Lizard"

19. A – Bob Kelly

20. D – Brian Elliot

DID YOU KNOW?

1. Pesky forward Bob Kelly was known by most fans as "Mad Dog," but he also went by several other monikers during his big league career from 1970-71 to 1981-82. Kelly was also known as "Hound Dog," "The Hound," "Mutt," "Muttley," "Machine Gun Kelly," "Scourge of the Red Army," and "Grass Fairy."

2. Agitating Flyers forward Don Saleski was known to teammates, fans, and coaches as "Big Bird" in the 1970s. Saleski was a 6-foot-3-inch right-winger who spent 1971 to 1979 in the City of Brotherly Love, which is the famous nickname for the city of Philadelphia. He was given the name because his wild mane of blonde hair resembled the Big Bird character from the famous *Sesame Street* children's television show.

3. Blueliner Philippe Myers has been given the nickname "Giraffe" by teammate Kevin Hayes. Myers, who stands 6 feet 5 inches, reminds Hayes of a giraffe. Myers made the Philly lineup as a regular in 2019-20 even though he went undrafted.

4. Former head coach Fred Shero was known by the Philadelphia faithful as "The Fog." This wasn't because of the famous "Fog Game" in the 1975 playoffs or because Shero walked around in a haze. He was simply given the nickname because he was quite mysterious as he kept a

good distance away from his players other than at the rink. Shero coached the team to Stanley Cups in 1974 and 1975 and was later inducted into the Hockey Hall of Fame.

5. One of the best nicknames in all of hockey belonged to defenseman Larry Goodenough. His moniker was simply a play on words as he was affectionately known as "Izzy." This, of course, posed the question "Izzy Goodenough?" The rearguard was good enough to help the Flyers win their second consecutive Stanley Cup in 1975.

6. Power forward John LeClair made a name for himself with the Flyers by becoming the first American-born NHL player to rack up three straight seasons of 50 goals or more. He went by the nickname "Johnny Vermont" since he hailed from St. Albans, Vermont. LeClair banged in 51 goals in 1995-96 and followed that with seasons of 50 and 51.

7. LeClair, with center Eric Lindros and right winger Mikael Renberg, formed the famous "Legion of Doom" forward line with Philadelphia. They played together from 1995 to 1997 and were known for their highly physical play on the ice as well as their offensive prowess. All three were a minimum of 6 feet 2 inches in height and weighed at least 230 lbs.

8. Center Ron Flockhart was coined with the nickname "Flockey Hockey" because he had a penchant for carrying the puck all the way up the ice rather than passing it. He played with Philadelphia in the early 1980s and posted 72

points on 33 goals and 39 assists as a rookie in 1981-82. He hit his peak early but did register three more seasons of at least 20 goals.

9. The heavily bearded Flyers forward Bill Flett was known throughout the NHL simply as "Cowboy." The native of Alberta, Canada, was given the nickname because he really was a cowboy. Flett lived on a farm and competed in rodeos during the offseason. He was the best-scoring cowboy in the NHL in 1972-73, when he banged in a career-high 43 goals.

10. The Flyers franchise is often known as the "Philly Flyers," but the name most associated with it is "The Broad Street Bullies." In 1972-73, the rugged team steamrolled over the Atlanta Flames in a brawl-filled game. The headline in the *Philadelphia Bulletin* on January 3, 1973, read, "Broad Street Bullies Muscle Atlanta." The phrase was created by writers Jack Chevalier and Pete Cafone, and it has stuck ever since.

CHAPTER 5:

THE CAPTAIN CLASS

QUIZ TIME!

1. The Flyers have had six players serve as captain for only one season.

   a. True
   b. False

2. Who has held the captaincy for the single longest consecutive period of time?

   a. Dave Poulin
   b. Eric Lindros
   c. Claude Giroux
   d. Bobby Clarke

3. How many captains have the Flyers had?

   a. 9
   b. 18
   c. 20
   d. 15

4. On January 23, 2000, the Flyers traded Rod Brind'Amour, Jean-Marc Pelletier, and a 2nd round pick, and in return received which future team captain?

   a. Keith Primeau

   b. Eric Desjardins

   c. Mike Richards

   d. Keith Jones

5. Which Flyers captain appeared in eight All-Star Games?

   a. Claude Giroux

   b. Dave Poulin

   c. Bobby Clarke

   d. Eric Lindros

6. Eric Lindros tallied 115 points in the 1995-96 season, eclipsing his previous total of 70 points.

   a. True

   b. False

7. In which season did captain Mel Bridgman record more than 190 penalty minutes and a +51 rating?

   a. 1981-82

   b. 1979-80

   c. 1980-81

   d. 1983-84

8. During the shortened 2012-13 season, Claude Giroux signed with Eisbären Berlin of the German DEL league before play in the NHL resumed and was named Philadelphia's next captain.

a. True

b. False

9. Rick Tocchet holds the record for most penalty minutes in franchise history. How many minutes did the one-time captain serve?

a. 1,800

b. 1,815

c. 1,920

d. 1,779

10. Who was the oldest player to hold the captaincy for the Flyers?

a. Ed Van Impe

b. Ron Sutter

c. Jason Smith

d. Chris Pronger

11. Captain of the Flyers from 1981 to 1983, Bill Barber leads the franchise in what three categories?

a. Assists, goals, shorthanded goals

b. Hat tricks, shots, assists

c. Shots, goals, even-strength goals

d. Assists, plus/minus, even-strength goals

12. The Flyers went without a captain for the 1994-95 season.

a. True

b. False

13. Ron Sutter holds the highest scoring percentage in a single season with the Flyers. What was it?

a. 24.5%

b. 24%

c. 23.8%

d. 22.9%

14. In a 12-2 win over the Detroit Red Wings, how many goals did Bobby Clarke score?

a. 4

b. 6

c. 3

d. 7

15. How many game-winning goals did Bill Barber score in the 1975-76 season?

a. 7

b. 8

c. 10

d. 12

16. Every captain of the Flyers has worn at least two different jersey numbers for the team.

a. True

b. False

17. Who was captain Dave Poulin traded for in 1989-90?

a. Jiří Látal

b. Ken Linseman

c. Kevin Maguire

d. Pete Peeters

18. How many years was Eric Lindros captain of the Flyers?

    a. 8

    b. 4

    c. 5

    d. 6

19. How many Flyers captains have scored at least 100 points in a season?

    a. 3

    b. 5

    c. 2

    d. 1

20. The Flyers have had how many captains (with at least five seasons playing for the club) enter the Hockey Hall of Fame?

    a. 3

    b. 4

    c. 1

    d. 2

QUIZ ANSWERS

1. A – True

2. C – Claude Giroux

3. B – 18

4. A – Keith Primeau

5. C – Bobby Clarke

6. A – True

7. C – 1980-81

8. A – True

9. B – 1,815

10. D – Chris Pronger

11. C – Shots, goals, even-strength goals

12. B – False

13. A – 24.5%

14. C – 3

15. C – 10

16. B – False

17. B – Ken Linseman

18. D – 6

19. A – 3

20. A – 3

DID YOU KNOW?

1. Philadelphia has had 18 captains between 1967 and 2020, starting with Lou Angotti in their inaugural year. He was followed by Ed Van Impe, Bobby Clarke, Mel Bridgman, Bill Barber, Dave Poulin, Ron Sutter, Rick Tocchet, Kevin Dineen, Eric Lindros, Erik Desjardins, Keith Primeau, Derian Hatcher, Peter Forsberg, Jason Smith, Mike Richards, Chris Pronger, and Claude Giroux.

2. Bobby Clarke took over as captain from Bill Barber in December 1972. Clarke was captain from 1972 to 1979 but had to give up the C after the 1978-79 season because he became a player-coach. Clarke served as captain again from 1982 to 1984. Ron Sutter took over as captain from Dave Poulin in December 1990, just before Poulin was traded to Boston. The team then went without a captain in 1992-93. Eric Desjardins took over from Eric Lindros in March 2000, when Lindros was stripped of the title, and Keith Primeau took over from Desjardins in October 2001, when Desjardins resigned the post. Derian Hatcher was named interim captain midway through 2005-06 when Primeau was sidelined for the season with a concussion.

3. Eric Lindros was stripped of the captaincy in 2000 after he publicly complained about the team's medical staff. His relationship with general manager Bobby Clarke had deteriorated at this point because Lindros suffered several

injuries and the GM questioned his toughness. Eric Desjardins was given the C, but he handed it back to the team in October 2000 because he said the pressure of being the captain was negatively affecting his game.

4. Bobby Clarke made it to the Hockey Hall of Fame despite suffering from diabetes. Clarke was the youngest captain in the NHL when the Flyers gave him the C at the age of 23 in 1972-73. He was skipper of the squad from 1973 to 1979 and again from 1982 to 1984. Clarke notched 358 goals and a club-high 1,210 points with the team in 1,144 regular-season games and spent his entire playing career with the club. He later became general manager and is currently the Flyers' senior vice president.

5. The youngest captain in team history was winger Eric Lindros, who was just 21 years old when given the honor in 1994-95. The oldest player to be named captain was defenseman Chris Pronger, who was 37 when given the C in 2011-12. Pronger was captain for just 13 games because he was injured early in the season, but the Flyers didn't name a replacement captain until the following season.

6. Many fans may have forgotten about Lou Angotti, who was the first-ever Philadelphia captain when the club debuted in the NHL in 1967-68. The 30-year-old Angotti was acquired in the 1967 NHL Expansion Draft from the Chicago Blackhawks with the 33rd overall pick. The forward played just one season in Philadelphia and posted 12 goals and 49 points in 70 regular-season games.

7. Bill Barber captained the Flyers for just over one season but finished his career as the team's all-time leader in goals, with 420. He played his entire 12-year career with the Flyers. Barber scored 883 points in his 903 regular-season games and added 53 goals and 108 points in 129 postseason outings. He scored 50 goals in 1975-76 and had four seasons of at least 30 goals and another four of at least 40 goals. Barber notched 30 goals as a rookie and never fell below the 20-goal mark in any season. He retired in 1985 following knee surgery. His jersey was retired by Philly, and he later became head coach.

8. Four former Flyers captains have been inducted into the Hockey Hall of Fame, but only three of them played with the club for more than five seasons. These were Bobby Clarke, Bill Barber, and Eric Lindros. Forward Peter Forsberg was captain in 2006-07 but played just 100 regular-season games with Philadelphia, while Chris Pronger was captain in 2011-12 and was with the team for 145 regular-season matches.

9. Forward Dave Poulin wasn't a flashy Flyers captain, but he was consistent and did a fine job. He took over as captain in 1985-86 and held the title for five and a half seasons. The Flyers reached the Stanley Cup Finals twice with Poulin as captain but lost to Edmonton both times. In 1983-84, he set a rookie scoring record for the team with 76 points and won the Frank Selke Trophy as the NHL's best defensive forward. Poulin tallied 394 points in 467 regular-

season games with the Flyers, including 27 shorthanded markers.

10. In 1992-93, the Flyers didn't name a captain but forward Kevin Dineen was given the honor the following season. He spent just over seven seasons with the Hartford Whalers to kick off his career before arriving in Philadelphia in a trade in 1991-92. He was an instant hit with the Broad Street Bullies, scoring 56 points in 64 games over the rest of the season. Dineen recorded just 42 points in his lone season as captain and two years later was dealt back to Hartford.

CHAPTER 6:

STATISTICALLY SPEAKING

QUIZ TIME!

1. Bobby Clarke recorded back-to-back-to-back seasons with a team record 89 in which statistical category?

   a. Points

   b. Goals

   c. Assists

   d. Shots

2. In 1989-90, Ron Hextall played a career-low 8 games and posted a career-worst goals-against average of?

   a. 4.15

   b. 3.15

   c. 4.30

   d. 3.25

3. Who led the Flyers with 22 points and 13 goals to help the team win its first Stanley Cup in 1973-74?

   a. Bobby Clarke

   b. Ross Lonsberry

c. Rick MacLeish

d. Tom Bladon

4. Reggie Leach is the franchise leader for goals in a single season with 57.

    a. True

    b. False

5. How many penalty shot goals did Simon Gagne score in 2008-09?

    a. 3

    b. 4

    c. 2

    d. 5

6. In 674 games played, Jakub Voráček has climbed the franchise ladder to 6th place in assists with how many?

    a. 412

    b. 395

    c. 400

    d. 393

7. The Flyers have won 157 games all-time against which division rival?

    a. New York Rangers

    b. Pittsburgh Penguins

    c. New Jersey Devils

    d. Washington Capitals

8. In 2006-07, the Flyers scored a franchise low in points of how many (with a minimum of 70 games played in a season)?

    a. 49
    b. 58
    c. 56
    d. 60

9. What is the highest number of Flyers team hat tricks scored in a combined regular and postseason?

    a. 5
    b. 6
    c. 14
    d. 9

10. What is the highest points-per-game average in a single season by Eric Lindros?

    a. 1.49
    b. 1.60
    c. 2.00
    d. 1.58

11. Ron Hextall became the first goaltender to score in a playoff game.

    a. True
    b. False

12. Claude Giroux leads the Flyers in games played, with 883.

    a. True
    b. False

13. Tim Kerr and Eric Lindros share the same goals-per-game average at?

    a. 0.54
    b. 0.62
    c. 0.60
    d. 0.50

14. The Flyers amassed a total of 1,532 points at the Spectrum from 1968 to 1996.

    a. True
    b. False

15. Until 2019, how many wins and losses did the Flyers have in the playoffs?

    a. 233 wins-200 losses
    b. 200 wins-233 losses
    c. 212 wins-221 losses
    d. 221 wins-212 losses

16. What is the greatest goals-per-game average in a single season for a Flyers player?

    a. 0.80
    b. 0.77
    c. 0.78
    d. 0.74

17. Ron Hextall's career save percentage was?

    a. .912
    b. .895

c. .900

d. .880

18. What is the highest point total posted by a Flyer in a single season?

   a. 111

   b. 107

   c. 120

   d. 123

19. How many penalty minutes did Dave Schultz serve in the 1975-76 season?

   a. 408

   b. 400

   c. 307

   d. 278

20. Bernie Parent has played 3 more games than Ron Hextall, making Parent the franchise leader in games played by a goalie.

   a. True

   b. False

QUIZ ANSWERS

1. C – Assists

2. A – 4.15

3. C – Rick MacLeish

4. B – False

5. C – 2

6. D – 393

7. B – Pittsburgh Penguins

8. C – 56

9. C – 14

10. D – 1.58

11. A – True

12. B – False

13. C – 0.60

14. A – True

15. D – 221 wins-212 losses

16. B – 0.77

17. B – .895

18. D – 123

19. C – 307

20. B – False

DID YOU KNOW?

1. Mark Recchi had the greatest individual point-scoring season by a Flyers player in 1992-93, when he posted 123 points on 53 goals and 70 assists in 84 regular-season games. Recchi enjoyed a pair of stints with the team and scored 627 points in 602 regular-season contests with the club. The Hall-of-Famer also added 39 points in 65 playoff games.

2. As far as goaltending goes, the Flyers' top regular-season season performance was by Roman Čechmánek, who had a goals-against average of 1.83 in 2002-03. He also owns the 3rd and 4th best goals-against averages in team annals: 2.01 in 2000-01 and 2.05 in 2001-02. Čechmánek also had 20 shutouts, a 92.3 save percentage, and the best career goals-against average (over 150 games played) for the team at 1.96 in 163 regular-season games.

3. The Flyers have scored a total of 204 combined regular-season and postseason hat tricks. The record for most hat tricks in one season is five, by Tim Kerr in 1984-85. Kerr also holds the club record of 20 career hat tricks, followed by Rick MacLeish with 15. Eric Lindros and John LeClair had 12 each.

4. Power forward Tim Kerr was known as a power-play specialist, and the stats back that up. Kerr tallied an NHL record 34 goals with the man advantage in 1985-86 and

also led the team in that department on three other occasions. Kerr posted 144 power-play goals in 601 games with Philly, which still stands as the team record.

5. Kerr wasn't just able to score with the man advantage, though, as he also contributed 186 even-strength goals for a total of 363 to rank 3rd all-time for the franchise. His career-high for goals in a regular-season season was 58, which he achieved twice, and he also scored 54 goals twice. He also had 287 assists for Philadelphia for 650 points in 601 outings.

6. Philadelphia's most dangerous penalty killers over the years have been Bobby Clarke, Bill Barber, and Dave Poulin, who are all former team captains. Clarke scored 32 shorthanded goals for the time, while Barber had 31, and Poulin contributed 27. The regular-season high in Flyers history for shorthanded goals is seven, which is shared by Brian Propp, Mark Howe, and Mike Richards.

7. Winger Reggie Leach scored the most regular-season goals during a single campaign for the Flyers, with 61 in 1975-76. His 51 even-strength goals that season is also a club record. Leach also had a good year in 1979-80, when he scored an even 50. He currently ranks 7th all-time in Flyers goals with 306 in 606 contests. He added 208 assists for a total of 514 points.

8. The Broad Street Bullies have been awarded 65 combined regular-season and playoff penalty shots between 1967 and 2019-20 and have scored on 22 of them. Simon Gagne

leads the way with 3 penalty shot goals on three attempts, followed by Eric Lindros with 2 goals on two attempts. Bill Clement took the team's first attempt in 1974 and failed to score. Former captain Mike Richards leads the way with five penalty shots as a Flyer and was successful only once.

9. The Flyers were definitely known for their rough play, hence the Broad Street Bullies nickname. The player with the most career regular-season penalty minutes for the club is Rick Tocchet at 1,815, followed by Paul Holmgren at 1,600, Andre Dupont at 1,505, and Bobby Clarke at 1,453. They all played at least 500 games though. Dave Schultz skated in just 297 contests and is 5th on the list with 1,386 minutes.

10. The most successful head coach in franchise history was Fred "The Fog" Shero. He was behind the bench for 554 regular-season games between 1972 and 1978 and had a wins-losses-ties record of 308-151-95 for 711 points and a points percentage of 64.2. He also went 48-35 in the playoffs, won a pair of Stanley Cups with the squad, and was inducted into the Hockey Hall of Fame.

CHAPTER 7:

THE TRADE MARKET

QUIZ TIME!

1. Which future Vezina Trophy-winning goaltender did the Flyers trade in 2011-12?

   a. Sergei Bobrovsky

   b. Brian Elliot

   c. Steve Mason

   d. Mackenzie Blackwood

2. The Flyers made their first trade on September 1, 1967, with the Toronto Maple Leafs. Who or what did the trade involve?

   a. Art Stratton for Wayne Hicks

   b. Rick MacLeish for future considerations

   c. Al Millar for cash

   d. Al Millar for Rosaire Paiement

3. The Flyers sent six players, two 1st round draft picks, and $15 million to the Quebec Nordiques to acquire Eric Lindros.

a. True

b. False

4. Whom did the Flyers trade to acquire Darryl Sittler from the Toronto Maple Leafs?

    a. Tim Kerr

    b. Rich Costello

    c. Reggie Leach

    d. Brian Propp

5. The Flyers traded Bernie Parent to which Canadian team for two seasons?

    a. Quebec Nordiques

    b. Montreal Canadiens

    c. Toronto Maple Leafs

    d. Winnipeg Jets

6. The Flyers traded Peter Forsberg to the Nashville Predators and received which package in return?

    a. Scottie Upshall and a 2nd round draft pick

    b. Scottie Upshall, Ryan Parent, and a 1st and 3rd round draft pick

    c. Kimmo Timonen and a 1st and 2nd round draft pick

    d. Mikko Lehtonen, Ryan Parent, and a 1st round draft pick

7. The Flyers acquired Brayden Schenn, Wayne Simmonds, and a 3rd round draft pick from the Los Angeles Kings for which two players?

    a. Kimmo Timonen and Rob Bordson

    b. Jaromír Jágr and Daniel Brière

c. Mike Richards and Rob Bordson

d. Daniel Brière and Mike Richards

8. A 2012 trade saw defenseman Luke Schenn come to Philadelphia via Toronto in exchange for which young talent?

a. James van Riemsdyk

b. Tyler Bozak

c. Erik Gustafsson

d. Phil Kessel

9. The Flyers traded Simon Gagne to the Los Angeles Kings in 2011-12 for Wayne Simmonds.

a. True

b. False

10. Which player did the Flyers NOT receive from the Montreal Canadiens in the 1995 blockbuster deal that saw Mark Recchi leave Philadelphia?

a. John LeClair

b. Eric Desjardins

c. Gilbert Dionne

d. Kevin Dineen

11. Which player was reacquired by Philadelphia via trade in 1973 and greatly benefited the Flyers in the next two seasons upon his return?

a. Ron Hextall

b. Ed Van Impe

c. Dave Schultz

d. Bernie Parent

12. After playing with his father Gordie and brother Marty for the Hartford Whalers, Mark Howe was traded to the Flyers in 1982.

    a. True
    b. False

13. The Flyers traded forward Jeff Carter to which team before he was traded again to the Los Angeles Kings?

    a. New York Islanders
    b. Boston Bruins
    c. Columbus Blue Jackets
    d. Washington Capitals

14. During the 2018-19 season, when the Flyers used eight different goaltenders, how many of them were acquired in trades?

    a. 1
    b. 2
    c. 3
    d. 4

15. Philadelphia acquired two-way center Peter Zezel in a trade with the St. Louis Blues.

    a. True
    b. False

16. The Flyers dealt Justin Williams to the Carolina Hurricanes for which rugged player?

    a. Matt Martin
    b. Shawn Thornton

c. Colin White

d. Danny Markov

17. Who did the Flyers trade Al MacAdam, Larry Wright, and a 1st round draft pick for?

a. Paul Holmgren

b. Terry Crisp

c. Reggie Leach

d. Bob Stewart

18. Vincent Lecavalier played two seasons near the end of his career with Philadelphia before being traded to which team in 2015-16?

a. Los Angeles Kings

b. Tampa Bay Lightning

c. Florida Panthers

d. Dallas Stars

19. The Flyers unloaded Jeff Carter to the Columbus Blue Jackets for fellow forward Jakub Voráček and a 1st and 3rd round draft pick.

a. True

b. False

20. How many trades did the Flyers make during the 2018-19 season?

a. 13

b. 12

c. 16

d. 19

QUIZ ANSWERS

1. A – Sergei Bobrovsky

2. C – Al Millar for cash

3. A – True

4. B – Rich Costello

5. C – Toronto Maple Leafs

6. B – Scottie Upshall, Ryan Parent, a 1st and 3rd round draft pick

7. C – Mike Richards and Rob Bordson

8. A – James van Riemsdyk

9. B – False

10. D – Kevin Dineen

11. D – Bernie Parent

12. A – True

13. C – Columbus Blue Jackets

14. A – 1

15. B – False

16. D – Danny Markov

17. C – Reggie Leach

18. A – Los Angeles Kings

19. A – True

20. B – 12

DID YOU KNOW?

1. One of the biggest trades in Philadelphia history took place on January 31, 1971. The F`nst average. Bobrovsky won the Vezina Trophy as the NHL's best goalie in 2012-13 and 2016-17 and was named to the First All-Star Team both seasons.

2. One of the lowest-drafted goalies in Flyers history was Tommy Söderström, who was taken with the 214th overall pick in 1990. Söderström was just 5 feet 7 inches tall and weighed 157 pounds. He played two seasons with the Flyers from 1992 to 1994 and was then traded to the New York Islanders. The Flyers reacquired Ron Hextall and a 6th round draft pick in the 1995 steal of a deal. Söderström played 78 games for Philly, compiling an 88.6 save percentage and a 3.61 goals-against average.

3. The Sutter family was famous in the NHL beginning in the 1970s as six brothers all played in the league. The Flyers drafted Ron Sutter 4th overall in 1982, while Rich, his twin brother, went 10th overall to the Pittsburgh Penguins. However, just a year later, Rich was traded to Philadelphia in an eight-player trade. The Sutter twins played three seasons together with the Flyers from 1983-84 to 1985-86, and Ron later served as team captain for two seasons.

4. Another pair of brothers who wound up with the Flyers were Luke and Brayden Schenn. Blueliner Luke was

drafted 5th overall by Toronto in 2008 and acquired by Philadelphia in a deal for James van Riemsdyk in 2012. He played 213 regular-season games with Philly before being traded to Los Angeles. Center Brayden Schenn was also drafted 5th overall as Los Angeles took him in 2009. He was acquired by the Flyers in 2011 along with Wayne Simmonds and a 2nd round draft pick for Rob Bordson and former Flyers captain Mike Richards.

5. Forward Rick Tocchet was a 6th round draft pick by Philadelphia in 1983. A favorite of fans and management, he was named captain in 1991-92. However, it may have been a jinx as he wore the C for just 42 games before being traded. Tocchet went to Pittsburgh along with Kjell Samuelsson, goaltender Ken Wregget, and a 3rd round draft pick for future Hall-of-Famer Mark Recchi, Brian Benning, and a 1st round draft pick. Tocchet was then reacquired by the Flyers in March 2000 from Arizona for forward Mikael Renberg.

6. Center Eric Lindros caused a fuss in 1991 when he announced he wouldn't play for the Quebec Nordiques if they drafted him 1st overall. Quebec took him first anyway and was then stuck between a rock and a hard place. They agreed to send Lindros to Philadelphia for Peter Forsberg, Kerry Huffman, Steve Duchesne, Ron Hextall, two 1st round picks, and $15 million in cash. Hall-of-Famer Lindros served as the Flyers' captain for close to six seasons before being traded to the New York Rangers in 2001 for Jan Hlaváč, Kim Johnsson, Pavel Brendl, and a 3rd

round draft pick.

7. Peter Forsberg was an interesting part of the Lindros trade since the Flyers had drafted him 6th overall in 1991. He was traded to Quebec before playing a game with Philadelphia, but they would reacquire him in 2005 when they signed him as a free agent. Forsberg, who is also now in the Hockey Hall of Fame, was made team captain and scored 115 points with the Flyers in 100 regular-season games. He was traded in February 2007 to Nashville for Ryan Parent and Scottie Upshall along with a 1st and 3rd round draft pick.

8. Another future Hall-of-Famer ended up in Philadelphia when the Flyers gave up Ken Strong, the rights to Rich Costello, and a 2nd round draft choice to Toronto for center Darryl Sittler. The deal in 1982 appeared to be a steal for the Flyers because Strong and Costello were fringe players. Sittler produced 84 goals and 178 points for the Flyers in 191 regular-season games before being traded to Detroit in 1984 for Joe Paterson and Murray Craven.

CHAPTER 8:

DRAFT DAY

QUIZ TIME!

1. How many players did the Flyers draft between 1967 and 2019?

    a. 403
    b. 492
    c. 300
    d. 578

2. How many 1st overall draft picks have the Flyers had?

    a. 7
    b. 4
    c. 1
    d. 11

3. Who was the first player ever selected by the Flyers in the 1967 Amateur Draft?

    a. Brit Selby
    b. Lou Morrison
    c. Al Sarault
    d. Serge Bernier

4. How many goaltenders have the Flyers selected in the NHL Entry Draft?

   a. 62

   b. 70

   c. 44

   d. 15

5. Which defenseman was selected by the Flyers in the 1st round of the 2014 Draft?

   a. Ivan Provorov

   b. Robert Hagg

   c. Mark Friedman

   d. Travis Sanheim

6. Shayne Gostisbehere was drafted in which round of the 2012 Draft?

   a. 4th

   b. 3rd

   c. 2nd

   d. 5th

7. The Flyers had only five picks in the 2008 Entry Draft.

   a. True

   b. False

8. The Flyers have made only 30 draft picks in the 1st round.

   a. True

   b. False

9. How many defensemen have been drafted by the Flyers?

a. 143

b. 75

c. 158

d. 180

10. How many left wingers have the Flyers drafted?

a. 91

b. 85

c. 87

d. 90

11. The Flyers have drafted a total of 86 right wingers.

a. True

b. False

12. Ron Sutter was drafted in which round of the 1982 Entry Draft?

a. 6th

b. 2nd

c. 5th

d. 1st

13. In the 1967 NHL Expansion Draft, how many players did the Flyers pick from the Boston Bruins?

a. 4

b. 7

c. 2

d. 3

14. The Flyers have never obtained a 1st overall pick by winning the draft lottery.

    a. True
    b. False

15. How many centers have been drafted by the Flyers?

    a. 100
    b. 88
    c. 97
    d. 111

16. Which Flyer was selected 12th by the Las Vegas Golden Knights in the 2017 Expansion Draft?

    a. Nick Cousins
    b. Pierre-Edouard Bellemare
    c. Luke Schenn
    d. Ryan White

17. What year was Antero Niittymäki drafted by the Flyers?

    a. 2000
    b. 1997
    c. 1999
    d. 1998

18. What year was current team captain Claude Giroux drafted?

    a. 2005
    b. 2007
    c. 2004
    d. 2006

19. Legendary goaltender Ron Hextall was drafted by the Flyers in the 6th round in 1982. What overall draft pick was he selected with?

a. 119

b. 108

c. 112

d. 117

20. The Flyers did not select any players in the 1968 Draft.

a. True

b. False

QUIZ ANSWERS

1. B – 492

2. C – 1

3. D – Serge Bernier

4. A – 62

5. D – Travis Sanheim

6. B – 3rd

7. A – True

8. B – False

9. C – 158

10. C – 87

11. A – True

12. D – 1st

13. B – 7

14. A – True

15. C – 97

16. B – Pierre-Edouard Bellemare

17. D – 1998

18. D – 2006

19. A – 119

20. B – False

DID YOU KNOW?

1. The Flyers have had the 1st overall draft pick only once in their history, in 1975. They took center Mel Bridgman, who served as team captain for a short time. Bridgman played in Philadelphia from 1975 to 1981-1982 and racked up 119 goals and 324 points in 462 regular-season games, with 43 points in 74 playoff outings.

2. Philadelphia has also had the 2nd overall draft pick on two occasions. They chose winger James van Riemsdyk in 2007, and in 2017, they selected center Nolan Patrick. Van Riemsdyk notched 47 goals and 99 points for the club in 196 regular-season contests before being traded midway through the 2012-13 season to Toronto. Van Riemsdyk was reacquired in July 2018 as a free agent. He had 46 goals and 88 points in his first 132 outings upon his return. Patrick had registered 26 goals and 61 points in 145 regular-season games through the 2019-20 season.

3. The first player ever drafted by the team was winger Serge Bernier, who was selected 5th overall in 1967. Bernier played just one game for the club in both 1968-69 and 1969-70 before cracking the lineup the next season. He played 123 regular-season games with Philadelphia and scored 35 goals and 75 points.

4. One of the Flyers' most disappointing 1st round draft picks was winger Ryan Sittler in 1992. Sittler was the son of

former Flyer and Hall-of-Famer Darryl Sittler, and a lot was expected of him. However, the youngster never played an NHL game.

5. 4In 1978, the Flyers drafted winger Anton Stastny in the 12th round with the 198th overall pick. Anton was one of the famous Stastny brothers of Czechoslovakia, along with Peter and Marian. He contributed 636 points in 650 career regular-season games, but unfortunately, none of them came with Philadelphia. Anton played his entire career with the Quebec Nordiques because the NHL ruled he was too young to be drafted in 1978. He re-entered the draft the next year and was taken 83rd overall by Quebec.

6. The lowest-drafted Flyer who enjoyed a successful NHL career was goaltender Johan Hedberg, who was taken with the 218th choice in 1994. He played 373 career regular-season matches with a goals-against average of 2.82 and a 90.1 save percentage from 2000-2001 to 2012-13. Hedberg was another draftee who didn't play a game with the Flyers, though, because he was traded to San Jose for a 7th round draft pick in 1999.

7. The highest-scoring draft choice in Philly history was former captain and Hall-of-Famer Bobby Clarke. He was selected with the 17th overall pick in 1969 and ended his career with 358 goals and 1,210 points in 1,144 games. He added 42 goals and 119 points in 136 postseason games. Of the 18 captains in team history between 1967 and 2020, just 8 were originally drafted by the Flyers. The others were

acquired by trade or free agency, except for Lou Angotti and Ed Van Impe, who were chosen in the 1967 NHL Expansion Draft.

8. The Flyers selected Hall-of-Famer Bernie Parent 2nd overall from the Boston Bruins in the 1967 NHL Expansion Draft. Parent would win two Stanley Cups, Vezina Trophies, Conn Smythe Trophies, and First-Team All-Star selections with Philadelphia by 1975. The Flyers lost him for three seasons, but he was just 22 years old when drafted. Another Hall of Fame goalie went 1st overall in that 1967 Draft: Terry Sawchuk was taken by the Los Angeles Kings from Toronto. Sawchuk was already 38 years old, and he unfortunately passed away two years later.

9. Each of the expansion teams selected two goaltenders in 1967 along with 18 skaters. The Flyers took goaltenders Bernie Parent and Doug Favell; defensemen Ed Van Impe, Joe Watson, John Miszuk, Terry Ball, Dick Cherry, Dwight Carruthers, and Jean Gauthier; and forwards Brit Selby, Lou Angotti, Leon Rochefort, Don Blackburn, Garry Peters, Jim Johnson, Gary Dornhoefer, Forbes Kennedy, Pat Hannigan, Bob Courcy, and Keith Wright.

10. The 1967 Expansion Draft saw forward Gary Dornhoefer land in Philadelphia. The hard-hitting winger was taken in the 14th round with the 81st overall pick and played the rest of his career with Philadelphia. Dornhoefer displayed a decent scoring touch with 202 goals and 518 points in games with the Flyers along with 1,256 penalty minutes. He was inducted into the club's Hall of Fame in 1991.

CHAPTER 9:

GOALTENDER TIDBITS

QUIZ TIME!

1. What was Bernie Parent's save percentage in the 1974-75 playoffs?

   a. .910

   b. .924

   c. .915

   d. .899

2. How many times did Doug Favell win the Vezina Trophy with the Flyers?

   a. 0

   b. 3

   c. 1

   d. 2

3. What was Carter Hart's record in his rookie season?

   a. 15 wins-12 losses-3 overtime losses

   b. 16 wins-13 losses-1 overtime loss

c. 20 wins-10 losses-3 overtime losses

d. 20 wins-11 losses-5 overtime losses

4. In the 2018-19 season, Anthony Stolarz allowed 35 goals in 12 games played.

   a. True

   b. False

5. What was Martin Biron's goals-against average in 2007-08?

   a. 2.46

   b. 1.97

   c. 2.60

   d. 2.59

6. How many penalty minutes did Ron Hextall serve with the Flyers?

   a. 468

   b. 470

   c. 512

   d. 461

7. In 2013-14, Steve Mason had a career year with the Flyers, posting a record of 36 wins, 10 losses, and 7 overtime losses to win the Vezina Trophy.

   a. True

   b. False

8. Which Flyers netminder has the most assists in team history?

   a. Bernie Parent

   b. Ron Hextall

c. Brian Elliot

d. Bob Froese

9. Which Flyers goaltender with a minimum of 100 games played has the lowest save percentage at .879?

   a. Dominic Roussel

   b. Pelle Lindbergh

   c. Pete Peeters

   d. Ken Wregget

10. How many assists did Ron Hextall post in the 1988-89 season?

    a. 5

    b. 7

    c. 8

    d. 10

11. Brian Boucher played how many regular-season games with the Flyers?

    a. 174

    b. 277

    c. 290

    d. 389

12. The Flyers needed the services of emergency backup goalie Eric Semborski against the Chicago Blackhawks on December 3, 2016.

    a. True

    b. False

13. Bernie Parent's 271 wins tie him with Kelly Hrudey. They are ranked where on the all-time wins list in the NHL as of 2019-20?

    a. 47th
    b. 53rd
    c. 49th
    d. 50th

14. Ron Hextall holds the record for the most penalty minutes accrued by a goalie during his NHL career, with 569.

    a. True
    b. False

15. How many goaltenders have the Flyers used from 2010 to 2019-20?

    a. 17
    b. 15
    c. 12
    d. 18

16. Who had a career goals-against average of 1.96 with the Flyers?

    a. Brian Boucher
    b. Doug Favell
    c. Bernie Parent
    d. Roman Čechmánek

17. Which goalie won an even 50 regular-season games for the squad?

a. Robert Esche

b. Brian Elliott

c. Garth Snow

d. Rick St. Croix

18. How many NHL All-Star Game appearances did Bernie Parent make?

a. 6

b. 5

c. 4

d. 3

19. In 2010-11, rookie Sergei Bobrovsky started 52 games in net and placed 7th in Calder Trophy voting with what record?

a. 29 wins-12 losses-6 overtime losses

b. 27 wins-9 losses-8 overtime losses

c. 28 wins-13 losses-8 overtime losses

d. 30 wins-13 losses-4 overtime losses

20. In 1984-85, Pelle Lindbergh won the Vezina Trophy with a record of 40-17-7 and a .899 save percentage.

a. True

b. False

QUIZ ANSWERS

1. B – .924

2. A – 0

3. B – 16 wins-13 losses-1 overtime loss

4. A – True

5. D – 2.59

6. D – 461

7. B – False

8. B – Ron Hextall

9. D – Ken Wregget

10. C – 8

11. A – 174

12. B – False

13. C – 49th

14. A – True

15. D – 18

16. D – Roman Čechmánek

17. B – Brian Elliott

18. B – 5

19. C – 28 wins-13 losses-8 overtime losses

20. A – True

DID YOU KNOW?

1. Hall of Fame goalie Bernie Parent holds the team record for wins in a season with 47 in 1973-74 and also led the Flyers with 44 in 1974-75 and with 35 in 1976-77. Parent also posted a team-high 12 shutouts in 1973-74 and 1974-75 and had another 7 in 1977-78. He also holds the regular-season team records in saves (1,988), save percentage (93.2), shots against (2,159), losses (29), ties-shootout-overtime losses (20), minutes (4,307) and games played (73).

2. The worst career regular-season goals-against average for a netminder with at least 100 games was Ken Wregget. He posted a 3.55 goals-against average in 107 games between 1989 and 1992. His 87.9 save percentage is also the lowest for goalies who played at least 100 games. His record was much better than his statistics, though, as he went 42-47-9 with the team.

3. When it comes to puck-handling goaltenders, Ron Hextall was by far the best of the bunch. He posted 27 assists in 489 regular-season games and scored a goal against Boston in December 1987. He then became the first NHL goalie to score in the playoffs when he netted his second career marker in 1988-89 against the Washington Capitals.

4. Although the Flyers have been in the NHL since 1967, they don't hold many traditional goaltending records. Ron Hextall shares the record for one playoff goal with Martin

Brodeur and holds the mark for 569 regular-season penalty minutes in a career. Hextall also shares the records for most playoff losses in a season at 11 and most appearances in a playoff season at 26. He holds records for most penalty minutes in a season at 113, most penalty minutes in a playoff season at 43 and in career playoff games at 115.

5. Ray Emery appeared in 88 regular-season games with the Flyers, compiling a record of 35-34-10 between 2009 and 2015. He was acquired as a free agent in June 2009 and played one season before moving on. He then rejoined the team as a free agent in the summer of 2013 and stayed for two seasons before leaving once more. Emery passed away at the age of 35 in July of 2018 when he drowned in his hometown of Hamilton, Ontario.

6. The Flyers set a dubious NHL mark in 2018-19, when they used eight different goalies during the regular season. The team had used five on several occasions, but nobody had ever used more than seven. Philly set the milestone as Carter Hart, Brian Elliott, Anthony Stolarz, Calvin Pickard, Michal Neuvirth, Cam Talbot, Alex Lyon, and Mike McKenna all played at least one game.

7. The highest-drafted goalies in club history other than the 1967 NHL Expansion Draft were Maxime Ouellet and Brian Boucher, who were both taken in the 1st round with the 22nd overall pick. Boucher was chosen in 1995, and Ouellet was chosen in 1999. Boucher appeared in 328 career NHL games, while Ouellet played in only a dozen.

8. Brian Boucher ranks 6th on the all-time regular-season games played list for goalies with the Flyers, with 174 appearances. He went 73-68-19 with a goals-against average of 2.50 and a save percentage of 90.4, with 8 shutouts. Boucher played with the team from 1999-2000 to 2001-02 and was then traded to Arizona. He was reacquired by Philadelphia in July 2009 as a free agent and played another two seasons. He once again made his way back to the club in January 2013 via a trade with Carolina and played the last four games of his career with Philly.

9. The Flyers' Pelle Lindbergh was the first European to win the Vezina Trophy as the NHL's best goalie in 1984-85. He was named to the All-Rookie Team in 1982-83 and the First All-Star Team in 1984-85. Lindbergh played just over five years in the league before passing away. He led the Flyers to the Stanley Cup Finals in his third season where they were downed in five games by the Edmonton Oilers.

10. One of Philadelphia's most underrated netminders was Steve Mason. He was chosen as NHL Rookie of the Year in 2008-09 and was also named to the Second All-Star Team when he led the league with 10 shutouts with Columbus. Mason was traded to the Flyers in 2013 and played just over four seasons before signing with Winnipeg as a free agent in 2017. For goalies with over 100 games played, Mason ranks 3rd for the Flyers in regular-season games (231), 3rd in wins (104), 2nd in save percentage (91.8), 4th in goals-against average (2.47), and 5th in shutouts (14).

CHAPTER 10:

ODDS & ENDS

QUIZ TIME!

1. Among Flyers coaches who have been behind the bench for more than one season, which has the highest win percentage of .642 in the franchise's history?

    a. Pat Quinn

    b. Mike Keenan

    c. Dave Hakstol

    d. Fred Shero

2. On December 8, 1987, goaltender Ron Hextall scored his first NHL goal against which team?

    a. Boston Bruins

    b. Edmonton Oilers

    c. Pittsburgh Penguins

    d. Montreal Canadiens

3. From 1980 to 1993, the Flyers played in the Prince of Wales Conference.

a. True

b. False

4. How many members of the Flyers' organization have been inducted to the Hockey Hall of Fame?

    a. 16

    b. 17

    c. 19

    d. 15

5. Which Philly coach had a win-loss percentage of .609?

    a. Paul Holmgren

    b. Ken Hitchcock

    c. Pat Quinn

    d. Terry Murray

6. How many Flyers have been named to the NHL All-Rookie Team?

    a. 11

    b. 8

    c. 10

    d. 12

7. How many goals did the 1974-75 Flyers score in their playoff run?

    a. 46

    b. 47

    c. 50

    d. 53

8. In 1987-88, Rick Tocchet recorded 3 hat tricks.

    a. True
    b. False

9. Which team did the Flyers NOT face in the 2009-10 playoffs?

    a. Chicago Blackhawks
    b. Pittsburgh Penguins
    c. Montreal Canadiens
    d. New Jersey Devils

10. How many penalty shot opportunities have the Flyers had in franchise history?

    a. 71
    b. 60
    c. 65
    d. 59

11. The Flyers have scored on 33% of their penalty shot attempts.

    a. True
    b. False

12. How many shots did the four Flyers netminders face in the 1982-83 season?

    a. 2,203
    b. 2,136
    c. 2,109
    d. 2,145

13. The team used 34 different players in the injury-plagued 2005-06 season.

    a. True
    b. False

14. How many games did Bill Barber act as head coach of the Flyers?

    a. 145
    b. 140
    c. 130
    d. 136

15. What year were the Flyers assigned to the Metropolitan Division?

    a. 2014
    b. 2013
    c. 2012
    d. 2011

16. How many overtime losses did the Flyers have in the 2014-15 season?

    a. 12
    b. 15
    c. 18
    d. 20

17. What season did the Flyers have only 88 points but still reached the Stanley Cup Finals?

    a. 1979-80
    b. 1996-97

c. 2009-10

d. 1986-87

18. How many wins did the Flyers have in the 2012-13 campaign?

   a. 23

   b. 26

   c. 22

   d. 21

19. As the visiting team, which arena have the Flyers scored 419 goals in?

   a. Mellon Arena

   b. Great Western Forum

   c. Nassau Veterans Memorial Coliseum

   d. Madison Square Garden

20. Four Flyers are tied in 4th place for the most assists in a season with 68 assists each.

   a. True

   b. False

QUIZ ANSWERS

1. D – Fred Shero

2. A – Boston Bruins

3. B – False

4. C – 19

5. D – Terry Murray

6. A – 11

7. D – 53

8. A – True

9. B – Pittsburgh Penguins

10. C – 65

11. A – True

12. C – 2,109

13. B – False

14. D – 136

15. B – 2013

16. C – 18

17. C – 2009-10

18. A – 23

19. D – Madison Square Garden

20. A – True

DID YOU KNOW?

1. One of the oddest moments in Flyers history took place February 8, 1972, when goaltender Bruce Gamble suffered a heart attack during the first period of a game in Vancouver. Gamble didn't know what happened and played the entire game. When the Flyers arrived in Oakland shortly afterward, Gamble complained of chest pains, and when he went to the hospital, he was told about his on-ice attack. He never played another NHL game and sadly passed away at the age of 44 in December 1982 due to heart failure.

2. The Flyers had their own good luck charm starting in 1969 in the form of singer Kate Smith. Her recorded version of "God Bless America" was often played before home games instead of the national anthem. Smith even appeared on three occasions to sing the song live. The Flyers used the song only for select games and registered a successful wins-losses-ties mark of 100-29-5 when it was played before the faceoff.

3. The NHL's infamous "Fog Game" occurred in Game 3 of the Stanley Cup Final on May 20, 1975, when the Flyers traveled to Buffalo. The arena didn't have air conditioning, and fog began to form and rise above the ice because of the humidity. This made it difficult for fans and players to see, and the game was halted several times so players from

both teams could skate around the ice to dissipate the fog. To make matters more bizarre, a bat flew close to the ice surface and was knocked out of the air by the stick of Sabres forward Jim Lorentz.

4. Another infamous Flyers contest was held at the Philadelphia Spectrum on January 11, 1976, when the team hosted the Russian Red Army squad. It was one of the dirtiest international games ever witnessed. The Russians left the ice in protest during the first period when Philadelphia's Ed Van Impe wasn't assessed an elbowing penalty after apparently knocking Valeri Kharlamov unconscious. After several minutes, they returned to the ice after being reminded they wouldn't get paid. The Flyers went on to outshoot them 49-13 and won the game 4-1.

5. Hockey ran in the blood for Philly goaltending legend Ron Hextall. His father Bryan, Hall of Fame grandfather Bryan, and Uncle Dennis all played in the NHL. His dad played 549 regular-season games with several clubs games between 1962-63 and 1975-76, while his grandfather skated in 449 contests with the New York Rangers from 1936-37 to 1947-48. His uncle competed in 681 games from 1968-69 to 1979-80. Ron was the only Hextall to suit up with the Flyers.

6. There have been 21 head coaches in the history of the Flyers, starting with Keith Allen in 1967. The most recent being Alain Vigneault in 2019-20. In between, the

following have been behind the bench: Vic Stasiuk, Fred Shero, Pat Quinn, Bob McCammon, Mike Keenan, Paul Holmgren, Bill Dineen, Terry Simpson, Terry Murray, Wayne Cashman, Roger Neilson, Craig Ramsay, Bill Barber, Ken Hitchcock, John Stevens, Peter Laviolette, Craig Berube, Dave Hakstol, and Scott Gordon.

7. The 1979-80 Flyers set a North American professional sports record by going 35 regular-season games without a loss. The squad, coached by Pat Quinn, saw its streak last from October 14, 1979, to January 6, 1980. During that stretch, the team won 25 times and tied 10 contests. They made it to the Stanley Cup Finals that season but were ousted in six games by the New York Islanders.

8. When the 2019-20 NHL season faced off, the Flyers were on their ninth general manager in franchise history with Chuck Fletcher in charge. Bud Poile had the job in their inaugural season in 1967-68 and was followed in succession by Keith Allen, Bob McCammon, Bobby Clarke, Russ Farwell, Bobby Clarke again, Paul Holmgren, and Ron Hextall. Allen was at the helm when the team won its two Stanley Cups, but they failed to make the playoffs under Farwell.

9. Nineteen former Flyers players and officials have been inducted into the Hockey Hall of Fame as of 2019. They are goaltender Bernie Parent; defensemen Allan Stanley, Paul Coffey, Chris Pronger, and Mark Howe; and forwards Bill Barber, Eric Lindros, Bobby Clarke, Adam

Oates, Peter Forsberg, Dale Hawerchuk, Mark Recchi, and Darryl Sittler. Those in the builders category are Keith Allen, Roger Neilson, Bud Poile, Pat Quinn, Fred Shero, and Ed Snider.

10. The Flyers also have their own Hall of Fame, which includes 25 members. The membership includes 20 former players and founder Ed Snider, former president Joe Scott, coach and general manager Keith Allen, coach Fred Shero, and broadcaster Gene Hart. The players are Bobby Clarke, Bernie Parent, Bill Barber, Rick MacLeish, Barry Ashbee, Gary Dornhoefer, Reggie Leach, Ed Van Impe, Tim Kerr, Joe Watson, Brian Propp, Mark Howe, Dave Poulin, Ron Hextall, Dave Schultz, John LeClair, Eric Lindros, Eric Desjardins, Rod Brind'Amour, and Jimmy Watson.

CHAPTER 11:

FLYERS ON THE BLUE LINE

QUIZ TIME!

1. Which Flyers defenseman scored 11 goals and 21 assists in the 1974-75 season?

   a. Tom Bladon

   b. Jimmy Watson

   c. Andre Dupont

   d. Ted Harris

2. How many assists did Mark Howe tally in his 10 years with the Flyers?

   a. 342

   b. 350

   c. 337

   d. 340

3. In the 1999-2000 season, four rearguards scored at least 50 points each.

   a. True

   b. False

4. How many points did Ivan Provorov post in his rookie season?

    a. 14
    b. 18
    c. 22
    d. 30

5. Who was the only Philly blueliner to play every game of the Flyers' inaugural season?

    a. John Miszuk
    b. Joe Watson
    c. Larry Zeidel
    d. Jean Gauthier

6. In 1981-82, Glenn Cochrane led the Flyers with how many penalty minutes?

    a. 314
    b. 265
    c. 329
    d. 342

7. Who was the first defender to score a goal for the Flyers on October 22, 1967?

    a. Larry Zeidel
    b. Dwight Carruthers
    c. Ed Van Impe
    d. John Hanna

8. Eric Desjardins played 738 games with the club, the 9th most in Flyers history.

a. True

b. False

9. How many assists did Kimmo Timonen have in the 2007-08 season?

   a. 13

   b. 8

   c. 40

   d. 36

10. How many assists did Flyers blueliners combine for during the 2009-10 playoffs?

    a. 38

    b. 42

    c. 26

    d. 31

11. The franchise-high +87 rating was recorded by a defenseman.

    a. True

    b. False

12. Paul Coffey played 94 games with the Flyers and tallied fewer points than he did in 60 games with the Los Angeles Kings.

    a. True

    b. False

13. How many points did Janne Niinimaa record in the 1996-97 season?

a. 44

b. 50

c. 40

d. 33

14. In the 1984-85 season, how many defensemen scored fewer than 30 points?

a. 2

b. 3

c. 5

d. 4

15. How many seasons did Hall-of-Famer Chris Pronger play in Philadelphia?

a. 1

b. 2

c. 3

d. 4

16. Which defenseman led the Flyers in time on ice in 2001-02, with 1,889 minutes?

a. Eric Weinrich

b. Kim Johnsson

c. Chris Therien

d. Dan McGillis

17. What was Barry Ashbee's team-leading plus/minus in the 1973-74 season?

a. 41

b. 46

c. 55

d. 53

18. How many defensemen suited up for the Flyers in the 2003-04 season?

    a. 11

    b. 15

    c. 12

    d. 14

19. Which blueliner tallied 17 points in the 1979-80 playoffs?

    a. Norm Barnes

    b. Mike Busniuk

    c. Bob Dailey

    d. Behn Wilson

20. Joni Pitkänen led the Flyers in goals with 39 during the 2006-07 season.

    a. True

    b. False

QUIZ ANSWERS

1. C – Andre Dupont

2. A – 342

3. B – False

4. D – 30

5. A – John Miszuk

6. C – 329

7. C – Ed Van Impe

8. A – True

9. D – 36

10. B – 42

11. A – True

12. A – True

13. A – 44

14. D – 4

15. C – 3

16. B – Kim Johnsson

17. D – 53

18. D – 14

19. C – Bob Dailey

20. B – False

DID YOU KNOW?

1. "Ash Can" was the moniker handed to Flyers defender Barry Ashbee because of his rugged play and last name. Ashbee suffered a severe eye injury in the 1973-74 playoffs and was forced to retire. His number 4 jersey was the first to be retired by the club, and he became an assistant coach. The 37-year-old Ashbee died in 1977 from leukemia, and the franchise hands out the annual Barry Ashbee Trophy to the squad's best blueliner in his honor.

2. Blueliner Shayne Gostisbehere enjoyed a great rookie season in 2015-16, when he was voted to the All-Rookie Team and placed 2nd in Calder Memorial Trophy voting for Rookie of the Year. He notched 17 goals and 46 points in just 64 games. His four regular-season overtime goals set a new high for an NHL rookie as did his 15-game point-scoring streak by a rookie defenseman.

3. Tom Bladon had a record-setting game with Philadelphia on December 11, 1977, when he scored eight points in a game on four goals and four assists. He was the first NHL defenseman to achieve the feat and just the fourth player in history to do it. Fellow blueliner Paul Coffey equaled the mark in 1986. The Flyers hammered the Cleveland Barons on Bladon's historic night, and he also set a league record for the highest plus/minus mark in a game at +10.

4. Since he spent 21 seasons in the NHL, the odds were good

that Hall-of-Famer Paul Coffey would spend some time in Philadelphia. Coffey was traded to the Flyers from the Hartford Whalers in December 1996. He totaled 55 points in 94 games, with 9 points in 17 postseason matches. Coffey was traded to Chicago for just a 5th round draft pick in June 1998 when he was 37 years old.

5. Hall of Fame defenseman Mark Howe is the all-time leading scorer for Flyers blueliners, with 138 goals and 480 points in 594 regular-season games and a plus/minus rating of +351. He led the NHL in that category in 1986-86, with +87. He added 53 points in 82 playoff games with the club. In case you didn't know, Howe is the son of the famous Hall of Fame right winger Gordie Howe.

6. Eric Desjardins currently holds the club record for goals by a defenseman in the postseason, with 14. The former Flyers captain also chipped in with 37 assists for 51 points in 97 playoff games with the team. During his career, he notched 23 goals and 80 points in 168 postseason contests. He posted 93 goals and 396 points in 738 regular-season games with the Flyers.

7. Andy Delmore's name doesn't come up often in discussions about all-time great Flyers rearguards. However, he holds the club record for goals in a playoff season with five. He scored five goals and two assists in 18 playoff games in the 1999-2000 postseason and was the first rookie defenseman in NHL history to notch a playoff hat trick. The undrafted Delmore played 95 regular-season

games with the team from 1998-99 to 2000-01, scoring seven goals and 22 points.

8. Doug Crossman holds the franchise mark for most power-play goals by a blueliner in the playoffs with six in his Flyers career. Crossman, Tom Bladon, and Chris Pronger share the record with three power-play goals in one postseason. The underrated Crossman was a fine playoff performer with Philly as he posted 31 points in 60 outings. He also had 193 points in 392 regular-season contests with the club.

9. Doug Crossman also shares the Philadelphia record for most points from the blue line in one playoff season at 18 with Chris Pronger. Crossman registered four goals and 14 assists in 26 games in 1986-87. Pronger had four goals and 14 assists when he equaled the mark in 23 games in 2009-10.

10. The Flyers were definitely known as one of the roughest and toughest NHL teams during the 1970s, so it's no surprise that the most-penalized defenseman in club history started out in that era. Andre "Moose" Dupont leads the squad in career regular-season penalty minutes for a rearguard at 1,505 minutes, which places him 3rd on the team's all-time list. Dupont played 549 games with the team and also served 306 minutes in 108 playoff games.

CHAPTER 12:

CENTERS OF ATTENTION

QUIZ TIME!

1. Eric Lindros put up career highs in goals and assists in 1995-96. How many games did it take Lindros to post 115 points?

    a. 60

    b. 73

    c. 75

    d. 64

2. How many power-play goals did Rick MacLeish score in the 1972-73 season?

    a. 25

    b. 17

    c. 22

    d. 21

3. Which Flyers center led the team in scoring three seasons in a row, from 2008-09 to 2010-11?

a. Jeff Carter

b. Mike Richards

c. Daniel Brière

d. Darroll Powe

4. All of the captains in Flyers history have been centers.

a. True

b. False

5. How many points did Pelle Eklund score in the 1986-87 playoffs?

a. 25

b. 26

c. 27

d. 28

6. What was Bobby Clarke's plus/minus rating during the 1975-76 season?

a. +79

b. +80

c. +83

d. +86

7. Rod Brind'Amour scored eight game-winning goals for the Flyers in 1997-98.

a. True

b. False

8. In 2010-11, Jeff Carter and Daniel Brière combined for how many goals?

a. 53

b. 58

c. 65

d. 60

9. Among the top 10 goalscorers in team history, 5 of them played center.

    a. True

    b. False

10. How many points did Flyers centers combine for in the shortened 2012-13 season?

    a. 73

    b. 80

    c. 56

    d. 67

11. Center and captain Lou Angotti led the way for the Flyers in their first season, with 49 points.

    a. True

    b. False

12. How many goals did Brayden Schenn score during his six seasons in Philadelphia?

    a. 99

    b. 110

    c. 109

    d. 113

13. What was Claude Giroux's faceoff percentage in the 2016-17 season?

    a. 56.9%
    b. 54.7%
    c. 57.2%
    d. 55.9%

14. Which center played 55 games and recorded 48 points and a plus/minus of +25 in 1988-89?

    a. Mike Bullard
    b. Ron Sutter
    c. Dave Poulin
    d. Peter Zezel

15. How many points did Mike Bullard score during the 1989-90 season?

    a. 58
    b. 60
    c. 64
    d. 70

16. In an eight-goal blowout over the Vancouver Canucks on New Year's Eve 1997, how many goals were scored by Flyers centermen?

    a. 3
    b. 4
    c. 5
    d. 6

17. How many regular-season penalty minutes did Eric Lindros serve as a Flyer?

    a. 890
    b. 850
    c. 946
    d. 970

18. How many points did Daymond Langkow contribute in the 1999-2000 regular season?

    a. 50
    b. 47
    c. 45
    d. 42

19. Peter Zezel was the only Flyers center (with a minimum of 70 games played) to not score at least 60 points in the 1985-86 season.

    a. True
    b. False

20. Mel Bridgman had 12 seasons in which he scored at least 40 points. How many seasons of his streak were spent in Philadelphia?

    a. 7
    b. 6
    c. 4
    d. 5

QUIZ ANSWERS

1. B – 73

2. D – 21

3. A – Jeff Carter

4. B – False

5. C – 27

6. C – +83

7. A – True

8. D – 60

9. A – True

10. A – 73

11. A – True

12. C – 109

13. D – 55.9%

14. B – Ron Sutter

15. C – 64

16. A – 3

17. C – 946

18. A – 50

19. A – True

20. B – 6

DID YOU KNOW?

1. Center Alan Hill played his entire career with the Flyers from 1976-77 to 1977-78 with a few stints in the minors. He produced 40 goals and 95 points in 221 games, with 19 points in 51 playoff outings. He hit his peak in his very first NHL game on February 14, 1977, when he scored two goals and added three assists against the St. Louis Blues in a 6-4 triumph. Hill set a new NHL record with this performance for the most points in an NHL debut.

2. Hall of Fame center Dale Hawerchuk made quite a name for himself with the Winnipeg Jets and was named the NHL's Rookie of the Year for 1981-82. Not many fans remember that he played the final 67 regular-season games of his career with the Flyers, though. Hawerchuk was acquired in March 1996 from St. Louis in a trade for Craig MacTavish. He notched 54 points in his 61 appearances with Philly and added 16 points in 29 playoff games.

3. Adam Oates was another Hall of Fame center who made a brief stop in Philadelphia. He was traded to the Flyers from the Washington Capitals in March 2002 as a rental player for Maxime Ouellet and 1st, 2nd, and 3rd round draft choices. Oates skated in just 14 regular-season games and posted three goals and 10 points, adding two assists in five playoff outings. He then walked away from the team

several weeks later as a free agent and signed with Anaheim.

4. In the 1973-74 playoffs, center Rick MacLeish led the league in scoring with 13 goals and 22 points. His performance helped the Flyers win the Stanley Cup for the first time, but goaltender Bernie Parent won the Conn Smythe Trophy as the most valuable player in the postseason. MacLeish had two stints with the team, scoring 328 goals and 697 points in 741 regular-season games, with a club-record 53 goals and 105 points in 108 playoff contests.

5. Jeff Carter was a clutch performer for the Flyers, as he showed in 2008-09 when he tied the club record for most game-winning goals at 12. Winger Brian Propp had set the mark in 1982-83. Carter had a career year that season with 46 goals and 84 points. He played 461 regular-season games with the team from 2005-06 to 2010-11; 38 of his 181 goals were game-winners.

6. As far as regular-season overtime goals are concerned, current team captain Claude Giroux leads the way with 11 and counting. The center winger had 44 total game-winners at the end of 2019-20 and had accumulated 257 goals and 815 points in 889 contests. He also had two game-winning goals in the playoffs, including one in overtime.

7. One of the greatest playoff performances in Flyers history came from center Daniel Brière. He caught fire in the 2009-

10 postseason, setting a team record with 30 points. Brière notched 12 goals and 18 assists in 23 games to lead the league and tallied 37 goals and 72 points in 68 career playoff outings with the club between 2007-08 and 2012-13.

8. Orest Kindrachuk will forever be remembered by NHL fans for possessing one of the most unusual names in its history as well as for his consistent play. The undrafted center was signed by the Flyers as a free agent in the summer of 1971 and was a key player on the team's two Stanley Cup-winning teams. Kindrachuk scored 79 goals and 260 points in 360 regular-season games and was a +117 with the team. He added 35 points in 69 playoff encounters.

9. Iron-man streaks show that a player is willing to play through aches and pains. Center Rod Brind'Amour holds the Flyers' mark for playing 484 consecutive games between February 24, 1993, and April 18, 1999. Brind'Amour played 633 regular-season games with the team, scoring 235 goals and 601 points in the regular season and another 51 points in 57 playoff outings. His son Skyler was drafted 177th overall by the Edmonton Oilers in 2017.

10. Ken "The Rat" Linseman spent a lot of his time on the ice agitating opponents but could also be depended on offensively. He holds the club record for points per game in the playoffs at 1.29. Linseman posted 53 points in 41 postseason outings and had 257 points in 269 regular-

season games. He achieved this while serving 135 minutes in penalties in the playoffs and 585 in the regular season with the team.

CHAPTER 13:

THE WINGERS TAKE FLIGHT

QUIZ TIME!

1. Which winger had the most goals in the 2008-09 season?

    a. Mike Knuble

    b. Joffrey Lupul

    c. Simon Gagne

    d. Scott Hartnell

2. Which winger had 134 penalty minutes, the 2nd most in the Flyers' inaugural season?

    a. Gary Dornhoefer

    b. Pat Hannigan

    c. Claude Laforge

    d. Brit Selby

3. Left winger John LeClair scored 51 goals in each of the 1995-96 and the 1996-97 seasons.

    a. True

    b. False

4. How many goals did Mark Pederson score in the 1991-92 season?

   a. 19
   b. 17
   c. 15
   d. 20

5. Which winger posted the most assists in a season, with 70?

   a. Ken Linseman
   b. Mark Recchi
   c. Jakub Voráček
   d. Brian Propp

6. Which Flyers winger scored 14 points in the 1984-85 playoffs?

   a. Murray Craven
   b. Ilkka Sinisalo
   c. Brian Propp
   d. Tim Kerr

7. Which winger notched 60 points in the 2013-14 season?

   a. Michael Raffl
   b. Matt Read
   c. Wayne Simmonds
   d. Jakub Voráček

8. The top three goalscorers in Flyers franchise history are wingers.

   a. True
   b. False

9. Mikael Renberg tallied how many goals in the 1993-94 season?

    a. 40
    b. 38
    c. 35
    d. 39

10. Who had a +36 rating in the 1998-99 season?

    a. Valeri Zelepukin
    b. Mike Maneluk
    c. Keith Jones
    d. John LeClair

11. The first penalty shot in Flyers history was scored by right winger Bill Flett on March 7, 1974.

    a. True
    b. False

12. Paul Holmgren had an even 200 penalty minutes in the 1976-77 season.

    a. True
    b. False

13. How many points did Murray Craven record in the 1990-91 season?

    a. 55
    b. 43
    c. 50
    d. 47

14. Jakub Voráček earned how many assists in the 2017-18 campaign?

    a. 57
    b. 61
    c. 65
    d. 54

15. How many power-play goals did Scott Hartnell bang in during the 2011-12 season?

    a. 16
    b. 20
    c. 13
    d. 10

16. Claude Giroux scored how many points as a winger in 2011-12?

    a. 99
    b. 88
    c. 93
    d. 85

17. Which player scored 9 game-winning goals in the 1977-78 season?

    a. Bill Barber
    b. Rick MacLeish
    c. Ross Lonsberry
    d. Bob Kelly

18. Which winger was a +10 and scored 21 points in the 2009-10 playoffs?

a. Claude Giroux

b. Ville Leino

c. Arron Asham

d. David Laliberte

19. How many points did Justin Williams score with the Flyers?

a. 106

b. 98

c. 120

d. 115

20. Before shifting to center, Claude Giroux would often play on the right wing.

a. True

b. False

QUIZ ANSWERS

1. C – Simon Gagne

2. A – Gary Dornhoefer

3. B – False

4. C – 15

5. B – Mark Recchi

6. D – Tim Kerr

7. C – Wayne Simmonds

8. A – True

9. B – 38

10. D – John LeClair

11. B – False

12. B – False

13. D – 47

14. C – 65

15. A – 16

16. C – 93

17. A – Bill Barber

18. B – Ville Leino

19. D – 115

20. A – True

DID YOU KNOW?

1. Winger Simon Gagne was an excellent contributor for the Flyers. He notched 20 goals and 48 points as a 19-year-old rookie and added two campaigns each of more than 20, 30, and 40 goals. He peaked at 47 in 2005-06, with a league-leading 33 at even strength. Gagne registered 535 points in 691 games with Philly and 47 points in 90 playoff games. He had 47 game-winners in the regular season, 2 overtime winners in the postseason and was successful on all 3 of his career penalty shot attempts.

2. Known for his goal-scoring prowess, winger John LeClair was a fan favorite who played on the "Legion of Doom" line with Eric Lindros and Mikael Renberg. LeClair scored 333 regular-season goals and 643 points in 649 games with the team and added 35 goals and 74 points in 116 playoff outings. He was also an excellent two-way player. The five-time All-Star led the NHL with +44 in 1996-97 and was +197 in his Flyers career.

3. Mikael Renberg, the other winger on the "Legion of Doom" line, had two stints with the Flyers. He was drafted 40th overall by the club in 1990 and was traded to Tampa Bay in the summer of 1997. However, Tampa traded him back to Philly just 16 months later, and he played another two seasons with the Flyers before being traded to Arizona. Renberg produced 296 points in 366

regular-season contests with the Flyers and added 34 points in 50 playoff games.

4. There was a lot of pressure on wingers Jan Hlaváč and Pavel Brendl when they joined the Flyers with defenseman Kim Johnsson in August 2001. The reason was that they were all acquired from the New York Rangers in a trade that saw former Philadelphia captain and future Hall-of-Famer Eric Lindros head to Manhattan. Hlaváč and Brendl played just a combined 81 regular-season games with the club though and posted 23 points between them.

5. Winger Kevin Dineen was a former Flyers captain who joined the club in November 1991 via a trade with the Hartford Whalers. He spent just over four years with the team before being dealt back to Hartford. In between, Dineen scored 88 goals and 176 points for the Flyers, with 10 points in 15 playoff games. What made him unique was the fact that his father Bill Dineen was Philadelphia's head coach from 1991 to 1993 while he played there.

6. Justin Williams earned the nickname "Mr. Game 7" for scoring 15 points in the seventh game of the NHL playoff series. He won three Stanley Cups and a Conn Smythe Trophy as playoff MVP. The winger was drafted 28th overall by the Flyers in 2000 but played just four seasons as he struggled under three different head coaches and dealt with injuries. Williams scored in his NHL debut and posted 115 points in 226 games with Philly but added just 6 points in 17 playoff contests.

7. After the 2019-20 regular season, winger Brian Propp was ranked as the 3rd highest scoring Flyer in club history. Propp was drafted by the team 14th overall in 1979 and scored 369 goals and 849 points for Philadelphia in 790 games, adding 52 goals and 112 points in 116 postseason encounters. He shares the record for most shorthanded goals in a season at 7 with Mark Howe and Mike Richards and shares the mark for 12 game-winning goals in a season with Jeff Carter.

8. Right winger Jakub Voráček was acquired from Columbus along with 1st and 3rd round draft choices in June 2011. He had tallied 168 goals and 561 points in 674 contests by the end of the 2019-20 regular season. Voráček rarely misses a game as he was absent just 22 times in his first 12 seasons in the NHL.

9. One of the toughest Flyers ever was winger Paul Holmgren, who played with the team from 1975-76 to 1982-83 and served as head coach from June 1988 to December 1991. Holmgren skated in 500 regular-season games and served 1,600 minutes in penalties, which ranks 2nd all-time for the franchise. He chipped in with 138 goals and 309 points in the regular season and an impressive 50 points in 67 playoff games, with another 181 minutes in penalties.

10. Winger Ross Lonsberry was sent to Philadelphia by Los Angeles in January 1972 in a seven-player trade, and it soon became obvious he was as dependable in both ends

of the rink. Lonsberry notched 144 goals and 314 points in 497 regular-season outings and posted a +154 to rank 15th in franchise history. He also added 44 points in 83 playoff games and rarely missed a game to injury-sickness during his career.

CHAPTER 14:

THE HEATED RIVALRIES

QUIZ TIME!

1. Which Western Division team did the Flyers eliminate in their first playoff series victory?

    a. Minnesota North Stars

    b. Chicago Black Hawks

    c. St. Louis Blues

    d. Atlanta Flames

2. What year did the Flyers engage in a line brawl with their old rival, the Washington Capitals?

    a. 2012

    b. 2014

    c. 2013

    d. 2015

3. At the end of the 2019-20 season, the Flyers had played the Ottawa Senators 99 times in the regular season.

    a. True

    b. False

4. On December 1, 1974, the Flyers hammered which now-defunct team 10-0?

   a. Minnesota North Stars
   b. California Golden Seals
   c. Atlanta Flames
   d. Kansas City Scouts

5. Which rival team has eliminated the Flyers from the playoffs five times?

   a. New Jersey Devils
   b. New York Rangers
   c. Pittsburgh Penguins
   d. New York Islanders

6. Eric Lindros was involved in a famous on-ice rivalry against which New Jersey Devils player?

   a. Ken Daneyko
   b. Scott Stevens
   c. Claude Lemieux
   d. Bobby Holik

7. How many times have the Flyers and the New York Rangers faced off in the playoffs?

   a. 8
   b. 12
   c. 10
   d. 11

8. The Flyers have played at least 300 games against the New York Rangers.

a. True

b. False

9. When was the first time the Flyers and Pittsburgh Penguins met in the regular season?

   a. October 19, 1967

   b. November 7, 1967

   c. October 17, 1967

   d. November 4, 1967

10. In their first two playoff appearances, which team eliminated the Flyers in back-to-back seasons?

    a. Oakland Seals

    b. Boston Bruins

    c. St. Louis Blues

    d. Los Angeles Kings

11. The Flyers faced off against the New York Rangers in the 2010 Winter Classic.

    a. True

    b. False

12. The Flyers' victory over the New York Rangers in the 1973-74 playoffs was the first time an expansion team beat an Original Six team in the postseason.

    a. True

    b. False

13. How many games did the Flyers win in their seven meetings with the Washington Capitals in 1986-87?

a. 3

b. 6

c. 5

d. 4

14. What was the final score in the Flyers' contest against the New Jersey Devils on December 10, 1983?

    a. 9-1

    b. 7-1

    c. 10-0

    d. 8-2

15. How many shutouts have the Flyers recorded against the Toronto Maple Leafs?

    a. 20

    b. 13

    c. 19

    d. 17

16. Which club did the Flyers meet in the 1975 playoff contest infamously dubbed the "Fog Game"?

    a. Toronto Maple Leafs

    b. Buffalo Sabres

    c. New York Islanders

    d. Minnesota North Stars

17. Which rivalry from the 1973-74 Stanley Cup Final did the Flyers renew in the 2010 playoffs?

    a. Boston Bruins

    b. Buffalo Sabres

c. Toronto Maple Leafs

d. New York Rangers

18. In 1997-98, Eric Lindros started a rivalry by almost starting a fight in an arena parking lot against a player belonging to which team?

a. Colorado Avalanche

b. Florida Panthers

c. Dallas Stars

d. Tampa Bay Lightning

19. How many points did the Flyers score in their four outings against the Washington Capitals in the 2001-02 season?

a. 5

b. 8

c. 6

d. 4

20. From 1974 to 1989, the Flyers held their rivals the Pittsburgh Penguins to a winless record of 0-39-3.

a. True

b. False

QUIZ ANSWERS

1. A – Minnesota North Stars

2. C – 2013

3. A – True

4. D – Kansas City Scouts

5. B – New York Rangers

6. B – Scott Stevens

7. D – 11

8. A – True

9. A – October 19, 1967

10. C – St. Louis Blues

11. B – False

12. A – True

13. C – 5

14. D – 8-2

15. C – 19

16. B – Buffalo Sabres

17. A – Boston Bruins

18. D – Tampa Bay Lightning

19. B – 8

20. A – True

DID YOU KNOW?

1. There's a natural rivalry between Philadelphia and the Pittsburgh Penguins because they both entered the NHL in 1967-68, play in the Metropolitan Division, and are located in the same state. In fact, the rivalry is known as "The Battle of Pennsylvania." Their first meeting was on October 19, 1967. Flyers goaltender Doug Favell earned the shutout in a 1-0 win, and the winning goal was scored by Bill Sutherland. The Flyers' record against Pittsburgh was 86-36-19 from 1967 to 1989.

2. The Flyers-Penguins rivalry didn't really heat up until Mario Lemieux arrived in Pittsburgh in 1984-85. The clubs found themselves in separate divisions in 1974-75 when the NHL realigned. Pittsburgh was placed in the Norris Division for the next seven years, but the rivalry was somewhat renewed when both teams played in the Patrick Division starting in 1981-82. The Flyers posted a 42-game unbeaten streak over the Penguins at the Spectrum in Philadelphia for almost 15 years, between February 1974 and February 1989.

3. The Flyers and Penguins met in Game 5 of the Patrick Division Final in Pittsburgh on April 25, 1989, and history was made that night. Lemieux tied two playoff records with 5 goals and 8 points in a 10-7 Penguins win. The 17 goals wasn't a league record, though, because the Los

Angeles Kings had downed the Edmonton Oilers 10-8 seven years earlier.

4. The longest NHL game in the modern era and 3rd longest of all-time also involved Philadelphia and Pittsburgh. Keith Primeau scored the winner at the 12:01 mark of the fifth overtime period to give the Flyers a 2-1 win. The game took place on May 4, 2000, in the fourth game of the Eastern Conference Semifinals. Pittsburgh had won both games in Philly, and the Flyers won Game 3 in overtime in Pittsburgh. They then made it four wins in a row as they took the series in six.

5. The 2006-07 season was one the Flyers would like to forget when it comes to their rivalry with Pittsburgh. Philadelphia lost all eight meetings with their rivals, and Penguins goalie Marc-Andre Fleury became the first netminder to beat a club eight times in a season since 1967-68. Philly has swept the season series on three occasions against Pittsburgh. They won all four games in 1980-81, all seven in 1983-84, and all four in 2014-15.

6. Another intense Flyers rivalry is with their fellow Metropolitan Division hopefuls, the New Jersey Devils. This rivalry is known as "The Battle of the Turnpikes." The Devils are based in Newark, New Jersey, which is accessed by the New Jersey Turnpike, while Philadelphia, Pennsylvania, is accessible from the Pennsylvania Turnpike. The cities are only about 25 miles apart, and both turnpikes connect at the state borders. New Jersey leads 3-2 in the team's playoff meetings.

7. The Flyers and New York Rangers are well-known adversaries and have been division rivals since 1974-75. As of 2019, the clubs had met 11 times in the postseason, and the Flyers hold a 6-5 edge in series victories. The cities are less than 100 miles apart. Contests between the teams are typically hard-hitting and very intense, and each club's fans create an extremely hostile environment for visitors who are brave enough to make the journey.

8. The Flyers and Washington Capitals have been rivals since the old Patrick Division in the 1980s. Washington's first-ever playoff series triumph was a three-game sweep over Philly in the opening round in 1983-84. That basically cemented the end of the line for Bill Barber and Bobby Clarke, two former Flyers captains and Hall-of-Famers, as they retired following the defeat. They were also basically the last two members of the original Broad Street Bullies era.

9. The Flyers blew a 3-1 series lead to Washington in the first round of the playoffs in 1987-88, when they lost Game 7 in overtime. However, Philadelphia avenged the defeat the following season by ousting the division champions. The rivalry was re-energized in the 2000s when Alexander Ovechkin arrived on the scene for the Capitals. It has now intensified even more since NHL realignment in 2013, and the nastiness has spilled over on the ice several times. The clubs have met five times in the playoffs, with Washington leading 3-2 in series wins.

10. It's just natural that the Broad Street Bullies and Big, Bad Bruins would be fierce rivals even though they play in different divisions. The rivalry peaked in the 1970s, when the underdog Flyers upset Boston in six games in the 1973-74 Stanley Cup Finals. They met again in the playoffs three years in a row from 1976 to 1978 then had to wait until 2009-10 to renew their rivalry. In 2010, the Flyers roared back to win the series in seven games after losing the first three. However, Boston swept the series the next season in the Conference Semifinals and won the Stanley Cup. Each franchise has won three of their six playoff meetings.

CHAPTER 15:

THE AWARDS SECTION

QUIZ TIME!

1. How many times has Eric Desjardins won the Barry Ashbee Trophy, which is awarded to the Flyers' best defender?

    a. 10
    b. 8
    c. 6
    d. 7

2. Bobby Clarke won both the Lou Marsh Trophy for best Canadian athlete and the Lionel Conacher Award for best Canadian male athlete in 1975.

    a. True
    b. False

3. What was the first trophy awarded to a member of the Philadelphia Flyers?

    a. Jack Adams Award
    b. Conn Smythe Trophy

c. Bill Masterton Memorial Trophy

d. Hart Memorial Trophy

4. Who was the last Flyers player to win a major NHL trophy, in 2010-11?

    a. Jeff Carter

    b. Ian Laperrière

    c. Chris Pronger

    d. Eric Wellwood

5. How many times have the Flyers won the Clarence S. Campbell Bowl in back-to-back seasons?

    a. 6

    b. 2

    c. 3

    d. 4

6. The Flyers have never won the President's Trophy, which is awarded to the NHL team with the most regular-season points.

    a. True

    b. False

7. Who was the last coach of the Flyers to win the Jack Adams Award?

    a. Ken Hitchcock

    b. Terry Murray

    c. Mike Keenan

    d. Bill Barber

8. Ron Hextall won the Conn Smythe Trophy in 1986-87, becoming the fourth player to win the playoff MVP while on a losing team.

   a. True
   b. False

9. Who was the last Flyers goaltender to win the Vezina Trophy?

   a. Sergei Bobrovsky
   b. Ray Emery
   c. Pelle Lindbergh
   d. Steve Mason

10. Who won the Bill Masterton Memorial Trophy in 1988-89?

   a. David Poulin
   b. Tim Kerr
   c. Mark Howe
   d. Brian Propp

11. In what year was Mark Recchi inducted into the Hockey Hall of Fame?

   a. 2017
   b. 2015
   c. 2016
   d. 2018

12. Vic Stasiuk won the Jack Adams Award the first year the trophy was handed out to the best coach in the NHL.

   a. True
   b. False

13. Bob Froese shared the William M. Jennings Trophy with which other goaltender in 1985-86?

    a. Ron Hextall
    b. Glenn Resch
    c. Pelle Lindbergh
    d. Darren Jensen

14. Which Flyer took the Ted Lindsay Award home in 1994-95?

    a. Rod Brind'Amour
    b. John LeClair
    c. Michael Renberg
    d. Eric Lindros

15. How many different major NHL trophies did Bobby Clarke win?

    a. 3
    b. 5
    c. 4
    d. 6

16. Who was the first Flyer to be sent to the All-Star Game in 1968?

    a. Leon Rochefort
    b. Lou Angotti
    c. Bernie Parent
    d. Gary Dornhoefer

17. How many All-Star Games did Bobby Clarke play in?

a. 9

b. 8

c. 6

d. 7

18. After being traded back to the Flyers by the Toronto Maple Leafs, Bernie Parent won back-to-back Vezina and Conn Smythe Trophies while leading the Flyers to the Stanley Cup.

    a. True

    b. False

19. Which year was Flyers broadcaster Gene Hart honored with the Foster Hewitt Memorial Award for his 28 years of calling games?

    a. 1998

    b. 2000

    c. 1997

    d. 1999

20. How many team and individual trophies have been awarded to the Flyers organization?

    a. 42

    b. 50

    c. 39

    d. 41

QUIZ ANSWERS

1. D – 7

2. A – True

3. C – Bill Masterton Memorial Trophy

4. B – Ian Laperrière

5. C – 3

6. A – True

7. D – Bill Barber

8. A – True

9. C – Pelle Lindbergh

10. B – Tim Kerr

11. A – 2017

12. B – False

13. D – Darren Jensen

14. D – Eric Lindros

15. C – 4

16. A – Leon Rochefort

17. B – 8

18. A – True

19. C – 1997

20. A – 42

DID YOU KNOW?

1. Since their inception, the Flyers have won two Stanley Cups, six Clarence S. Campbell Bowls, and four Prince of Wales Trophies as conference champions. The squad led the National Hockey League in points three times in the regular season before the birth of the President's Trophy in 1985-86, but they haven't led the league in that category since 1984-85.

2. Philadelphia players and coaches have been awarded numerous trophies. They include the Bill Masterton Memorial Trophy (3), Conn Smythe Trophy (4), Frank J. Selke Trophy (2), Hart Memorial Trophy (4), Jack Adams Award (4), Lester Patrick Trophy (8), the NHL Plus/Minus Award (3), Ted Lindsay Award (2), Vezina Trophy (4), and the William M. Jennings Trophy (2). The Plus/Minus Award no longer exists, and the Lester Patrick Trophy is a joint award by USA Hockey and the NHL to recognize anybody's contribution to the sport in the USA.

3. The only Flyers to win the Hart Memorial Trophy as the NHL's Most Valuable Player are centers and former captains Eric Lindros and Bobby Clarke. Lindros won it for his play in 1994-95, while Clarke won in 1972-73, 1974-75, and 1975-76. Both players also won the Ted Lindsay Award for being voted by their fellow players as the best performer in the league. Clarke was honored in 1973-74 and Lindros in 1994-95.

4. The Conn Smythe Trophy, which is awarded to the most valuable player in the postseason, has been taken home by Flyers four times. Goaltender Bernie Parent shares a league record for winning it twice in a row, in 1973-74 and 1974-75, when the team won the Stanley Cup. Forward Reggie Leach won it in 1975-76 and netminder Ron Hextall in 1986-87 when the Flyers lost in the Stanley Cup Final.

5. As for goaltending, Bernie Parent won the Vezina Trophy as the NHL's top netminder for 1973-74 and 1974-75 and was a First-Team All-Star Team both of those seasons. Pelle Lindbergh won the Vezina in 1984-85, and Ron Hextall won it in 1986-87. Both were also First-Team All-Stars. Roman Čechmánek was a Second Team All-Star in 2000-01 as was Bob Froese in 1985-86. Froese and Darren Jensen shared the William M. Jennings Trophy in 1985-86 for giving up the fewest goals in the regular season; Čechmánek and Robert Esche shared it in 2002-03.

6. The Flyers have had their share of All-Star nominations for defensemen and forwards, too. Barry Ashbee was named to the Second All-Star Team once, while fellow defender Eric Desjardins made it twice, and Mark Howe made the First Team three times. At left wing, Bill Barber made the First Team once and the Second Team twice; Claude Giroux was a Second Team member once; John LeClair made the First Team twice and the Second Team three times. At center, Bobby Clarke made the First and Second Teams twice each, and Eric Lindros made them once each. At right wing, Tim Kerr, Reggie Leach, and Mark Recchi

were each named to the Second Team once, and Jakub Voráček made the First Team once.

7. The following Flyers have been named to the NHL All-Rookie Team: Pelle Lindbergh, Brian Boucher, and Ron Hextall as goaltenders; Thomas Eriksson, Shayne Gostisbehere, Janne Niinimaa, Joni Pitkänen, and Chris Therien as defenseman; and Simon Gagne, Eric Lindros, and Mikael Renberg as forwards.

8. Let's not forget the team's head coaches. Flyers coaches have won the Jack Adams Award four times for the coach of the year. Fred Shero was the first to win it for the 1973-74 season. He was followed by Pat Quinn in 1979-80, Mike Keenan in 1984-85, and Bill Barber in 2000-01.

9. Some top NHL awards have never been won by a Flyer. Mark Howe placed second in voting for the James Norris Trophy as the NHL's best defenseman three times. Bill Barber, Ron Hextall, and Shayne Gostisbehere all placed second in voting for the Calder Memorial Trophy as Rookie of the Year. Eric Lindros and Jaromír Jágr of Pittsburgh tied for the league scoring lead in 1994-95, but the Art Ross Trophy went to Jágr because he scored more goals. Also, no Flyer has won the Lady Byng Memorial Trophy for sportsmanship, gentlemanly conduct, and playing ability.

10. Notable NHL records shared by Flyers include most consecutive Conn Smythe Trophies; goaltender Bernie Parent has two. Reggie Leach shares the mark for most

playoff goals in a season with 19. Leach also scored five goals in a playoff game to share the record with four other players. Tim Kerr shares the record for the most goals in a period and most goals in a playoff period, with four. He also holds the record for most power-play goals in a season at 34 and most power-play goals in a playoff period and game at 4. Bill Barber is tied for most shorthanded goals in a playoff series and season with three.

CONCLUSION

There you go. You've just read through more than a half-century's worth of amazing Philadelphia Flyers facts, trivia, and statistics. We hope you've been entertained and, perhaps, you've learned something new about the franchise at the same time.

Most fans of the Broad Street Bullies probably know a good deal about their favorite team's players, coaches, and management already, but there may be something in the book that is new to you. If this is the case, then we're glad to have helped increase your knowledge.

Trivia, facts, statistics, and stories are never-ending, and there's always something new to add every day. There's nothing like challenging your fellow Philly Flyers fans to see who's the king of the hill when it comes to the team's trivia. You may also want to use the book to help convert fans of other NHL clubs.

Creating your own Flyers quiz can be fun and entertaining since we'd need hundreds of pages to include everything. Perhaps you can come up with some questions and facts that aren't included here to challenge other fans.

The history of the Philadelphia Flyers is quite intriguing, and the club will forever be known as the first expansion team to hoist the coveted Stanley Cup. The players, coaches, and management of this amazing franchise are unforgettable, and there are plenty of good times ahead.

The team has some of the most loyal and passionate supporters in all of sports. Thank you for being among them.

Made in the USA
Middletown, DE
13 December 2023